THE MIXELLANY GUIDE TO GIN

THE MIXELLANY GUIDE TO

GIN

GERALDINE COATES

MIXELLANY LIMITED®

Mixellany books may be purchased for educational, business, or sales promotional use. For information, please write to Mixellany Limited, 3 Eyford Cottages, Upper Slaughter, Cheltenham GL54 2JL United Kingdom or email jaredbrown1@mac.com

Second Edition

ISBN 13: 978-1-907434-28-0

British Library Cataloguing in Publication Data.
A catalogue record for this book is available from the British Library.

CONTENTS

INTRODUCTION

Gin, in that marvellous phrase of Lord Kinross writing in the 1930s, has been described as "an ardent spirit which rose from the gutter to become the respected companion of civilised man". Almost every step of that climb is connected to some aspect of British social history from the experiences of plague victims in the thirteenth century when The Black Death stalked Europe to the triumph of the Bloodless Revolution, from the building of a great Empire to the rediscovery of London as the capital of the world.

This book is an ode to gin, the basis for the most sophisticated drink of all time—the Dry Martini. Gin has a dual nature so glamour co-exists with images of drunkenness and despair hence "mother's ruin" or other names with negative associations whose origins are to be found in the well documented Gin Craze of the eighteenth century.

What is certain is that gin has always had its famous admirers, particularly amongst the reckless. Byron claimed that gin and water "is the source of all my inspiration" whilst F Scott Fitzgerald drank it because he believed it couldn't be detected on his breath. Faulkner, Hemingway, the Bright Young Things, the literati of the Algonquin Round Table, the Hollywood Rat Pack, the Rolling Stones and many more have a story about gin. But it is gin's own story that is the most compelling and I hope you enjoy it.

—Geraldine Coates

ACKNOWLEDGMENTS

Over the years many people have helped my gin journey by sharing their knowledge, writings and passion. Here are a few of them—Nick Blacknell, Jared Brown. Jake Burger, Patrick Dillon, Simon Ford, Lesley Gracie, Patience Gould, Craig Harper, Sean Harrison, Christopher and James Hayman, Joanne McKerchar of The Diageo Archive, Charles Maclean, Charles Maxwell, Anistatia Miller, Xavier Padovani, Desmond Payne, Luca Picchi, Gary Regan, Audrey Saunders, Nick Strangeway, Angus Winchester, The bramble Boys, Tony Conigliaro, Luke Tegner, Ivano Tonutti, and many others.

WHAT IS GIN?

Once upon a time, gin could be simply described as clear, unaged ethyl alcohol re-distilled or rectified with a range of berries, herbs, roots and spices, known collectively as the "botanicals". Of these, juniper is, and pretty much always has been, the principal flavouring agent.

Nowadays, it's slightly more complicated in that, for the first time in 300 years and quite rightly, there is a proper definition of London Gin designed to protect the tradition and craftsmanship attached to the "London dry style". This has given rise in turn to more rigorous definitions of "gin" and "distilled gin". At its most simple this is how they work:

London Gin: Does not have to be made in London, but must be made in a traditional still by re-distilling higher quality than standard neutral alcohol (aka: base spirit) with only natural flavourings (aka: botanicals). No artificial flavourings can be added after distillation. Indeed, the only other substances that can be added after distillation are additional base spirit, water and a small amount of sweetening (not more than 0.5 grammes per litre of finished product). London Gin cannot be coloured. Typical London Gins are Beefeater, Gordon's, Hayman's, Tanqueray, and Whitley Neill.

Distilled Gin: Made in a traditional still by re-distilling neutral alcohol in the presence of natural flavourings. Additional natural or artificial flavourings may be added after distillation, as can other approved additives such as colouring. Typical distilled gins are new-wave gins like Hendrick's Gin, the London Gin, and Martin Miller's Gin.

Gin: Often known as "cold-compounded", is made from any type of suitable ethyl alcohol (usually a molasses spirit) and does not have to be re-distilled, rather the flavourings are simply stirred into the spirit. The flavourings can be artificial and additional sweetness, colours as well as other additives are also allowed. In practice no gin aficionado is seriously interested in this type of gin, but it's useful to know about it especially when one is asked why a bottle of supermarket-own label costs half as much as a reputable brand.

What sometimes causes confusion with these definitions is they are not based on how the final gin tastes. Taste is highly subjective which is why almost every official spirit definition is based on how the spirit is produced. Think whisky, rum, brandy, cognac, and even vodka.

THE SPIRIT

The best gins will always bear the description "London Gin" or "Distilled Gin" on the labels. Another sign of quality is the specified use of "100 percent grain spirit". The quality of this spirit is crucial to the final taste of the gin. A clean fresh grain spirit will always makes its presence felt; in fact it is the heart of a properly made gin.

The base spirit used in gin is made in a large column still known as a Coffey still after Aeneas Coffey, a Dublin excise officer. He patented his simple but effective design, in 1831, but in fact his "invention" was an improvement on a continuous still that had been the brainchild of Robert Stein, a Scottish whisky distiller, in 1827. Around this time, designs for continuous stills popped up all over Europe and were soon being exported to the Caribbean and other spirit producing regions.

There are many advantages to continuous distillation: a lighter, cleaner, more consistent spirit can be made in large quantities and the final strength of the spirit can be accurately specified. Importantly, continuous distillation is much more cost effective than having to pass grain alcohol through a pot-still several times to achieve the desired result.

Continuous distillation works on a very simple principle, common to all distillation, that water and alcohol boil at different temperatures. When an alcohol-bearing liquid is heated, the alcohol will separate and rise as a vapour, which, when it cools, reverts back to liquid that can then be collected. Most continuous stills consist of two linked columns—the analyser and the rectifier. Alcohol bearing liquid in the form of a fermented wash is fed into the top of the rectifier. It runs down, via a pipe, to the bottom of the column and up to the top of the analyser, where it then starts to descend. Meanwhile steam enters the bottom of the analyser and rises slowly up through a series of horizontal perforated plates to heat the cool liquid. As the steam and liquid travel across the plates the alcohol, in vapour form, is separated out. It is then captured in a condenser where it cools and becomes liquid again. The beauty of the system is that the distiller can collect the spirit at whatever strength he wants by adjusting the plates to capture the higher alcohols. In the case of gin, a high-strength, low-flavour spirit is required and so the spirit may be re-distilled until it has become an almost completely flavourless spirit at around 96 percent ABV.

A curious hangover from the bad old gin days is that, in the UK, the base spirit and the rectified spirit—that is, gin—must not be produced in the same location. This is the result of an Act of 1825, one of the many Gin Acts of the late eighteenth and early nineteenth centuries that were intended to control the trade and regulate quality so unscrupulous distillers could no longer make any old rubbish and re-distill it into gin. As a result, although modern gin distillers often get their neutral grain spirit from sister companies within their huge production empires, Tanqueray and Gordon's Gin, for example, must use grain spirit made at one part of Diageo's Scottish production facility, which is then transported to the other end of the site to be made into gin. Other companies get their spirit from independent producers like the Greenwich Distillery in London.

THE BOTANICALS

It's often been claimed that gin is "history in a glass". Nowhere is this more obvious than when one considers the abundance of exotic berries, roots, peels, seeds, and barks that are found in a simple tot of our favourite spirit. And it's no coincidence that gin and its Dutch ancestor genever—both flavoured with juniper berries, spices, and herbs—are the national drinks of two great seafaring nations with fleets that travelled the world bringing back weird and wonderful foodstuffs from the East and West Indies.

It would be hard to exaggerate just how important spices have been in Europe since time immemorial. Frustratingly though, for centuries, even millennia, the trade was almost entirely controlled by Arab and North African middlemen who protected the tortuous routes by which spices travelled from their places of origin in the East. They jealously guarded their sources even inventing fantastic stories such as the one that cassia grew in shallow lakes guarded by fierce winged animals! This sales pitch met with incredulity from the earliest times with Pliny the Elder (AD 23–79) commenting sarcastically: "All these tales…have been evidently invented for the purpose of enhancing the price of these commodities."

In the tenth century, Europe began to get in on the spice action with the powerful city-states Venice and Genoa prospering by importing spices from the Levant and selling them at vast profit in Europe. A war between the two cities, in 1398, saw Venice victorious, but, whilst everyone knew where the spices grew, for the next hundred years no one could break the Venetian monopoly on the trade routes. Towards the end of the fifteenth century however, European navigational science developed dramatically and it became possible to sail further and further afield. The race was on to get to the spice producing countries and trade directly with them. No wonder when one considers that nutmeg was more valuable than gold and people could pay their rent with pepper. There followed two centuries of exploration, war, and invasion all in pursuit of the fabled spices of the Orient. Along the way great European colonial empires were established all over the world but they were by-products of the desire for domination of the spice trade, not its original purpose.

In 1492, the Spanish Royal House funded Christopher Columbus's quest to find a new route to the East by sailing west across the Atlantic. He discovered the New World but died believing he had reached China. Vasco Da Gama, the great Portuguese explorer and navigator, reached India by sailing around the Cape of Good Hope, in 1498, and set up trading posts that allowed Portugal to dominate trade with India for a century. In the early 1600s, the English and the Dutch established their own East India Companies to build a network of outposts all over the

Far East to trade in spices and other goods, often using brutal tactics. By the seventeenth century, the Dutch and the English pretty much controlled the spice trade: Indeed it was often the cause of war between them. One such skirmish was resolved when England gave Holland the Banda Islands, where nutmeg grew, in return for a minor Dutch possession—Manhattan Island in the New World.

THE BOTANICALS USED IN GIN

The botanicals make gin gin and their use can be directly traced to the knowledge of herbalists and wise women in the days when medicine was in its infancy and people understood through centuries of experimentation the properties of what grew wild and used them to cure all manner of ailments.

Each gin recipe has a slightly different botanical mix and, whilst distillers may talk about the botanicals they use, their actual proportions are trade secrets and never revealed. However we can safely say that most gins will contain juniper, coriander, angelica and citrus in the form of lemon peel and orange peel (some gins, like Tanqueray TEN, use fresh citrus fruit). Orris root is also usually an important part of the recipe. Very dry gins often contain a greater proportion of rooty substances such as liquorice and angelica. Whilst there are reputedly over one hundred and twenty botanical ingredients that can be used in gin, most gins confine themselves to no less than four and rarely more than twelve botanicals. There are of course exceptions: more of that later.

Below is a list of the botanicals likely to be found in gin, starting, of course, with juniper, the queen of them all.

Juniper Berries

The juniper berries found in gin are actually a type of pine cone derived from *juniperus communis*, a small, coniferous shrub that grows wild throughout the Northern Hemisphere.

Juniper (from the French *"genièvre"*) gives gin its name and that instantly recognisable bitter-sweet taste of pine, lavender, and camphor, but the medicinal applications of juniper have been known since the dawn of civilisation. The earliest recorded medicinal use of juniper berries occurs in an Egyptian papyrus dating back to around 1500 BC, in a recipe to cure tapeworm infestations. Juniper berries have been found in Egyptian tombs where they were used as part of the embalming process. They were employed by both the Greeks and the Egyptians to ward off infections and this evolved into a belief, common throughout the Middle Ages, that the vapours from juniper berries could prevent leprosy and the bubonic plague. When the Black Death, a virulent form of bubonic plague, stalked Europe in the fourteenth century, killing over one third of the population, people even wore masks filled with juniper so that its aromas would protect them from the deadly disease. This folk medicine may well be rooted in therapeutic reality as juniper oil is still used in veterinary medicine to prevent fleas. (Oriental rat fleas carried by black rats were the vehicles that spread the bubonic plague.) In humans, oil of juniper was given to alleviate kidney and bladder infections as well as to treat indigestion and other digestive disorders.

Juniperus communis L

The juniper used in gin is carefully sourced with the best coming from mountain slopes in Italy and Macedonia. Once at the distillery, the berries are left to mature for anything up to two years until their oil is at its most aromatic. Because each year's crop will be slightly different, distillers will regularly test a number of samples to create the exact blend of berries they require. The proportion of juniper used in gin varies from recipe to recipe. Traditional gins use juniper as the keynote in their recipes and build all the other botanicals around it. In some new-style gins it is barely discernible.

Almond

Almond trees grow all over southern Europe. An important item of trade in the Middle Ages, almond oil is still used in medicines and skin care preparations. The bitter almond, not the sweet, is used in gin. First ground to release their oil, almonds impart a marzipan-like sweetness and softness to gin's complexity.

Angelica Root

According to legend, an angel revealed that angelica could cure the plague and for centuries it was also believed to guard against witchcraft. Almost all gin recipes will include shredded angelica root as not only does it make dry gin dry, it has woody, earthy notes that help to create an integrated botanicals profile.

Angelica Seed

Angelica seeds are widely used in traditional folk and Chinese medicines and are also found in many liqueurs that started life as herbal remedies. In gin, their fragrant, slightly musky notes complement the taste of juniper. Distillers in the past sometimes substituted angelica seeds for juniper when the latter was hard to source particularly because angelica grows wild profusely throughout the UK.

Bergamot Peel

There is an increasing fashion to broaden out the citrus profile in gin by including bergamot peel, derived from the fruit of the bergamot, a citrus mainly grown in Italy. In the eighteenth century, bergamot was used to flavour snuff, gin, and of course, the famous Earl Grey tea, so there is provenance here. Bergamot's musky, perfumed aromas are now found in a number of relatively new gin arrivals (see the chapter titled "Gin Brands" for details).

Cardamom Pods

The word itself sums up the exoticism of the Far East. After saffron and vanilla, cardamom is the third most expensive spice in the world. Before distillation, cardamom pods are crushed to allow the full flavour of the little black seeds inside to emerge. Cardamom brings warm, spicy, aromatic flavours to gin.

Caraway Seeds

Another member of the parsley family, caraway is native to Europe, Asia, and North Africa but is now widely cultivated throughout the world. Like coriander, the caraway "seed" is actually a ripe, dried fruit. It looks very much like cumin and is often mistaken for it. Caraway has been used in medicine for centuries. The Egyptians first recommended it as a digestive aid and antiflatulant in about 1500 BC. It is still used in babies' gripe water. In ancient Greece it was rumoured that the oil was an excellent therapy for pale-faced girls! Caraway is an extremely common cooking ingredient in Germanic countries where it is used to flavour rye bread and liqueurs such as kümmel.

Cassia Bark

Cassia bark comes from the cassia tree, which is native to Sri Lanka and China. In flavour and appearance it is very similar to its close cousin, cinnamon, but is more bitter. Think of Dentyne chewing gum and you'll recognise the taste—sharp and pungent, almost medicinal.

Cinnamon Bark

Another word that conjures up images of faraway tropical places, cinnamon is the bark of cinnamon tree and is generally ground to a fine powder before it enters the still. A pinch goes a long way as its warm, sweet, woody flavours can easily overpower.

Chamomile

Chamomile is a creeping plant that commonly forms daisy-like lawns throughout Europe, Asia, Australia, and the USA. In ancient Egypt chamomile was dedicated to the gods. Its name comes from the Greek for "ground apple" due to its distinctive scent. In Spain chamomile is called *manzanilla*, meaning "little apple". It's also the name of a light Spanish sherry, either because chamomile may once have been used to flavour it or because the sherry is reminiscent of its aroma. In Anglo-Saxon times chamomile was one of the "Nine Sacred Herbs" and was used widely in beer making until hops took over. In the Middle Ages, it was used as a "strewing" herb, spread on floors to make rooms smell sweeter. Chamomile is still a favourite garden herb, used in herbal infusions, chamomile "teas", and aromatherapy for its soothing and calming properties.

Coriander Seed

Coriander leaves and seeds are an essential ingredient in many Eastern cuisines. Its flavour has been prized for centuries. It is believed that the Romans introduced coriander to Britain as a meat preserver. In the eighteenth century, it was commercially grown in England. Coriander seeds have always made up a crucial part of the gin recipe. They are really tiny fruits that, during distillation, release spicy sage and lemon flavours, contributing a dry, peppery finish to a well-made gin. Distillers often source their coriander from southern Europe and North Africa. But nowadays a lot of coriander for gin comes from India.

Cubeb Berries

Cubeb berries are the fruit of the cubeb plant, a cardamom-like tropical vine that is a member of the pepper family. It has small white flowers that develop into tiny reddish brown seeds or berries. Cubeb is native to Indonesia. It came to Europe via India through Venetian trade with the Arabs. It was once used in herbal remedies and was believed to have aphrodisiac qualities. It became a popular substitute for the vastly more expensive black pepper in the Middle Ages.

Elderflower

Elder trees are common throughout Europe and grow wild in northern temperate regions. In folklore the elder tree is a symbol of grief because the Crucifixion cross was made from its wood. It was also believed to be the tree from which Judas hanged himself. The elder has magical associations throughout Europe: It is widely believed that burning elder wood brings bad luck but that elder sprigs hung inside provide protection from witches.

Both elderflowers and elderberries are used in cookery as well as to make wines and cordials. Elderflower is also used in Chinese medicine. Elderflower water was used in the eighteenth century to whiten the skin and remove freckles!

The best commercially grown elderflower comes from Southern Germany where the small yellowish white flowers of the elder are gathered in spring and early summer and dried carefully before they are put into the still with the other botanicals. Elderflower has a complex, distinctive, sweet smell that imparts fresh, herbal, floral notes with an acrid fruity undertone. Some people describe this as the aroma of white grapes, others as cat's pee.

Ginger

Ginger is the rhizome of *Zingiber officinale*. It is used either in root or powder form in different cuisines as well as in distillation. Ginger is a staple of Chinese traditional medicine and was mentioned in the writings of Confucius. It was also one of the earliest spices known in western Europe. Modern-day ginger ale and ginger beer evolved from tavern keepers' nineteenth-century custom of leaving out small containers of ground ginger for people to sprinkle into their beer. Ginger imparts dry, spicy flavours to gin.

Lemon Peel

Medicinally prized for its high vitamin C content, lemon juice was once given daily to sailors serving on Royal Navy ships to prevent scurvy. In gin, dried lemon peel—like other citrus fruit such as orange, lime, and grapefruit—adds a crisp, sharp bite that enhances the juniper flavour. Some gins have a stronger citrus profile than others, particularly more traditional gins. But it's rare to find one that does not include citrus in some form.

Liquorice

The root of the liquorice plant is widely used in the treatment of bronchitis. It's a common ingredient in cough medicines. Gin distillers often source their liquorice from the Middle East. It contains sugar, bitter compounds, and a substance that produces a characteristic woody, sweet flavour. Liquorice also softens and rounds out gin's mouth-feel.

Meadowsweet

Meadowsweet is a perennial herb that grows profusely throughout Europe, the eastern USA, and Canada. It has sweet smelling white flowers and slightly almond smelling leaves. It was one of the three herbs considered to be sacred by the Druids. It's mentioned in the "Knight's Tale" in Chaucer's *Canterbury Tales* as an ingredient of a drink called "Save". In Elizabethan times meadowsweet flowers were added to herb beers and wines; the leaves were placed into claret cups. It was also a popular Elizabethan strewing herb.

An excellent digestive remedy, meadowsweet is also an important source of salicylic acid, the basis of aspirin: the modern day wonder-drug whose name is derived from the old botanical name for meadowsweet—*spiraea ulmaria*. Its herbal, sweet, floral character enhances the freshness and zestiness of gin.

Orange Peel

In gin, dried orange peel gives fresh clean citrus notes that provide a counter note to the more pungent botanicals. Some gins, like Beefeater, use the bitter type of orange also known as Seville. Others such as Plymouth use a sweet orange.

Orris Root

Orris is the rhizome of the Florentine iris plant, dried and ground to a fine powder. It is found in talcum powder, perfumes, potpourri mixes, as well as in the delicate spice mix—*ras-el-hanout*—used in North African and Lebanese cooking. Aromatic and floral in itself with a hint of Parma violet, in gin, orris acts as fixing agent, holding the volatile elements of the other aromatics together.

HARVESTING THE BOTANICALS

Nothing about the cultivation and harvesting of most gin botanicals is remotely industrial—it's all done by hand the way it has always been, usually in places where it would be impossible to introduce machinery anyway. This is a direct throwback to the early days of medicine where herbalists foraged locally for plants and berries to prepare food and medicinal potions.

Take three core botanicals for example: juniper, orris and lemon peel. The best juniper berries, the ones all distillers want, grow wild at altitude and the best of the best come from the hills of Tuscany in a micro-climate situated between the sea and the Apennine Mountains. The berries take three years to ripen and are carefully gathered by local country folk who have the rights to harvest juniper on common land.

Using hand-made wooden baskets with a stout wire mesh—a bit like a soil riddle—they position the baskets under the branches and carefully beat the bushes with a wooden stick so that the berries fall into the baskets. The trick here is to gather only the ripe blue-black berries, leaving the green unripe ones to mature further until next year. It is hard work. Each harvester can pick only around 50 kilos of berries a day. But a more invasive, faster method would run the risk of losing next year's harvest. And that would be a disaster. Juniper is slow growing and once the bushes reach a certain age they stop producing fruit. Local people know the ways of juniper and play their part in ensuring that the right conditions exist for the next generation.

Tuscany is also home to fields of Florentine iris. *Iris Fiorentina* is grown commercially not for its flowers as some species of iris are, but for its rhizomes—underground root stems which, when dried, ground, and aged, go into the still as orris root, one of the most important of the gin botanicals.

First, the plants are dug out of the ground with a long-handled hoe in such a way as not to damage them. The rhizome chunks are carefully broken off leaving a small section attached to the plant to be replanted for next year's harvest. The plants take three years to mature before they can be harvested so it's crucial that the supply is maintained.

Then the rhizomes are peeled by hand using lethal, very sharp, curved knives. The peeled lumps of orris are scrubbed in water and put on wire racks to dry for fifteen days. At this stage they are virtually odourless. It takes months of ageing before they are able to release those delicate flavours of Parma violet and tea that are so distinctive in gin.

Harvesting orris is a genuine cottage industry and one can see the whole family, even children, sitting outside in the sunshine at the end of the day peeling and scrubbing just as Italian farmers might have done 500 years ago.

The same applies to the citrus harvest. Many distillers like Bombay Sapphire and Beefeater source their lemon peel in Murcia in southern Spain where a warm and sunny climate near the sea, sheltered by mountains, means that 80 percent of the region's agriculture is devoted to citrus growing. Here again it is a family affair with local farmers maintaining the tradition of producing top quality fruits. The lemons and oranges are peeled by hand before being left in long spirals to dry naturally in the Spanish sunshine.

It's reassuring somehow that, in an age of factory farming and chemically enhanced foodstuffs, all over the world from the jungles of Sri Lanka to the rainforests of Java to the mountains of Tuscany small family businesses are still devoting their expertise over generations to the production of these ingredients which of course are not only just found in gin but also in herbal remedies, perfumes, kitchens and a host of other applications.

MARRYING THE SPIRIT WITH THE BOTANICALS

London gin and distilled gin—henceforth to be known as "premium gin" for simplicity's sake—are made by re-distilling the base spirit with botanicals in a traditional pot-still. Making premium gin is a craft. Distillers all have their own ways of doing things according to their own traditions and how they want their gin to taste. The main difference in the production process nowadays lays between the "one shot method" and the "two shot method".

The One Shot Method

For many gins, the distillation process starts with charging copper pot-stills with neutral grain spirit, water, and the botanicals in the exact proportions of the recipe. The mix is then distilled and finally water is added to reduce it to bottling strength.

The Two Shot Method

Gordon's, Tanqueray, and many other gins use the two-shot method in which the botanicals are measured into the still at twice the strength of the recipe. Once the distillation is complete, additional spirit and water are added to achieve the proportions of the original recipe: a practice that conforms to the "London gin" definition. The advantage of course is that twice the amount of gin can be made in a single distillation, which is probably why most big brands use this method.

TO STEEP OR NOT

Some distillers leave the mix to steep in the still either overnight or longer before distillation. It's a more time consuming and hence costlier process but they believe that this maceration allows for a fuller extraction of flavour from the botanicals and the capture of a wider range of the more volatile oils. Others don't steep because they believe maceration stews the flavours of the botanicals. I have yet to meet the person who could identify which gins have been steeped and which have not by tasting the final result so one is left with the conclusion that the decision is part of each brand's unique history and production.

THE STILLS

M ost gin stills are onion shaped copper pot-stills exactly the same as the ones used to make malt whisky. They have elongated "swan" necks to extract the more fragrant, more volatile elements of the spirit. Each will have a condenser beside it to cool the alcohol bearing vapour back to liquid.

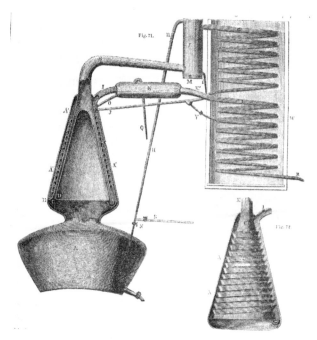

A copper pot-still design from the 1800s.

Copper is used in pot-stills because it dissolves easily and removes sulphury or vegetable aromas by chemical reaction. The shape of the pot-still has a major influence on the ultimate flavour of gin, as it will dictate the speed at which the spirit vaporises and begins to embed the botanical aromas. Indeed, when one of the stills at the Diageo plant (where Gordon's and Tanqueray are made) had to be replaced, the still-makers were instructed to copy the original still exactly even down to replicating dents and bashes. At the Blackfriars Distillery in Plymouth, the oldest working gin distillery in the country, the 160-year-old still has a shorter neck than normal and a steeper curve in the lyne pipe. Why? Because that's the way it's always been and because Sean Harrison Master Distiller at the Plymouth distiller believes that this design contributes to his gin's full bodied character.

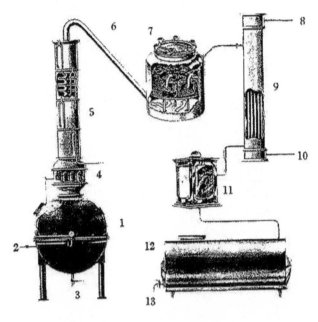

A *Carterhead column still.*

The other main type of still is called a Carterhead, developed in the nineteenth century by the two Carter brothers, who were originally employed by Aeneas Coffey. The Carterhead still was developed to further rectify the spirit produced by the Coffey still or column still. It employs the infusion or "steaming" method, once called "racking" in which the botanicals are carefully layered in a copper basket at the end of the lyne pipe at the very top of the still. When the spirit meets the botanicals it is therefore in vapour form and embeds the flavours as it returns to liquid.

IN THE STILL

Actual distillation starts when the stills are gently heated and the botanical-infused spirit begins its journey from liquid to vapour, crossing over the high swan neck of the still and returning to liquid, now gin, in the condenser. A distillation usually takes about seven to eight hours. It's a mysterious process, with each botanical releasing its flavour at different point in the cycle. First come the foreshots, those unwanted elements of the run, that are quickly discarded. Citrus elements emerge, then juniper and coriander, followed by rooty botanicals such as orris, angelica, and liquorice. These combine to create a glorious mélange of aromas that fill the stillroom.

The speed at which the still is run is crucial. Too fast and all the flavours bundle up and cross over together in a rush. Too slow and undesirable elements of the spirit are picked up.

The last part of the run through the stills, the feints, is also discarded. Like the foreshots, the feints contain flavours that the distiller doesn't want. Deciding when to make the "middle cut", as it is called, is probably the distiller's most important job. And, although gin distilleries increasingly resemble intensive-care units with dials and computers softly humming (and it could all be probably done with the click of a mouse), every distiller will taste the liquid coming through the spirit safe until it has the characteristics of the original recipe. Only then is the heart of the gin diverted into the spirit receiver. The point at which this is done is also part of the secret. No two gins are cut at the same time.

One can make educated guesses however and it is clear that some gins are noticeably richer and heavier. This could be because they contain more rooty substances but also because they may have been allowed to gather heavier elements of the spirit at a later point of the run. Other gins are fresher and lighter because they are more citrus laden and will probably have been cut at a higher strength earlier on.

WATER

The final stage of production is to reduce the gin to its bottling strength with water. Water comprises around 50 percent of the average bottle of gin and so distillers use filtered, exceptionally pure water. Bottling strengths vary considerably with the minimum for all gin set at 37.5 percent ABV, under EU law, right up to Plymouth Navy Strength's stonking 57 percent ABV. Most experts agree that for a gin to be considered premium it must be bottled at least 40 percent ABV. Why, you may ask, when the gin will be served with a mixer or in a cocktail and so diluted considerably? Does it really matter? Yes, because the alcohol carries the complex flavours of the botanicals. Below 40 percent ABV some of the more volatile citrus elements and aromatic top notes in gin are lost.

TASTING GIN

It's pointless trying to explore a particular gin's character when it has already been made up into a mixed drink or cocktail as most of the subtle flavours will be literally drowned out by the other ingredients. Far better to copy the whisky buffs.

Get some proper nosing glasses as they allow you to swirl the spirit and gather the aromas around the rim where they are more easily detected. Pour a good slosh in so the glass is around a third full. Start by smelling the gin because the tasting process combines aromas detected by the nose with sensory information received on the tongue.

Smell is our most acute sense and our noses do the groundwork of identifying individual aromas. (That's why people who have heavy colds complain that they can't taste their food.) Take a good sniff and think about what you're smelling: the aromas most commonly associated with gin are fruit (citrus), floral (orris, rose petals), spice (coriander, ginger, cassia), pine (juniper), and earth (liquorice, angelica).

Then, reduce the sample to 20 percent ABV by adding the same amount of water as there is gin in the glass. At this strength the flavours held in the alcohol are released. Water is used because it does not distort flavours.

Traditionally there are only four basic primary tastes: sweet, sour, salt, and bitter. (Another one, umami, has been recently added to the list but since it rarely applies to gin, let's keep it simple). Generally these four tastes are detected by taste buds on different parts of the tongue: sweet by the tip of the tongue, sour/acidic on the upper edges, salt at the sides and bitter/dry at the back. So it's important to swirl each gin around your mouth to analyse which part of your tongue is being stimulated.

Here are a few basic guidelines to what we're looking for.

Sourness picked up on the upper edges of the tongue indicates larger amounts of citrus in the form of bitter orange or lemon peel. Sweetness is derived from sweet citrus, floral ingredients and from some nuts like nutmeg and almond. Spiciness from coriander is usually detected on the sides of the tongue. A drying sensation on the back of the tongue sometimes indicates strong juniper but can also mean that the gin contains a greater proportion of rooty substances such as angelica and liquorice. And remember, taste is highly subjective: "seaweed in a damp cave on the Isle of Jura" or "a bouquet of summer flowers", for one person, can be a faintly medicinal tang or a cloying sweetness to another.

A gin has complexity when every area of the tongue is stimulated. Texture and body (aka: the "mouth feel") are also important. It's noticeable that some gins are lighter on the palate, others oilier and more viscous. That relates to the botanicals used in the mix, at what stage the gin has been cut during distillation, and its alcohol content. What every distiller is aiming for is balance and smoothness: the alcohol should hold all the flavours of the botanicals in harmony and the botanicals should balance each other.

The finish, too, is another indicator of quality. It's more than just an aftertaste; it's a summary of the whole tasting experience. Ideally, a gin's distinctive flavours should linger smoothly in your mouth after swallowing for a medium to long time, without leaving any unpleasant residue.

DUTCH GENEVER

Gin is a direct descendant of Dutch genever. So the quest to trace its roots starts with examining the development of the Dutch national spirit. It's easy to forget that genever or jenever is just as important today in Belgium as it is in modern-day Holland. For centuries, what is now Holland was once part of the Low Countries, a large area of northern Europe that corresponds roughly today to Holland, Belgium, Luxembourg, and also once included parts of northern France. The region stretched from Dunkirk in the southwest to Schleswig-Holstein in the northeast, once one of the most densely populated areas of Europe. It was bitterly fought over for centuries with the Holy Roman Empire, Spain, and France all vying for control. These conflicts had a direct effect on the evolution of gin.

THE FIRST JUNIPER-FLAVOURED SPIRITS

Distilling to make alcohol goes back to the dawn of time but sadly there are very few names and almost no pack drills. The earliest recorded distillers were probably the Babylonians who, in the second millennium BC were known to use clay pots to extract small amounts of distilled alcohol through natural cooling for perfumes. Eight centuries before Christ the Chinese were making *sautchoo* from fermented rice alcohol, the Tatars were producing *arika* from fermented mare's milk, and the Singhalese were distilling arrack from coconut toddy.

Aristotle wrote of the practice of distilling seawater to produce drinking water. Around 300 AD records of distillation began to be written, notably by Zosimos of Panopolis who described the techniques of the fabled alchemist Maria the Jewess who is believed to have invented distillation. For centuries alchemy and distillation were inextricably linked in the quest to find the "philosopher's stone" a legendary alchemical substance believed to be capable of turning base metals into gold and silver. It was also believed to be an elixir of life for rejuvenation and a way to achieve immortality.

But, strangely enough given Islam's prohibition on drinking alcohol, the European tradition of distilling in an alembic still to make potable spirit almost certainly descended from the writings of Arab alchemists who had translated the earliest Greek and Roman texts. Jabir Ibn-Hayyan (721–815 AD), aka: Geber, in particular is credited with perfecting the alembic still, which was a crucial tool in his constant experimentation. (The words "alembic" and *"al-kohol"* are Arabic).

In the ninth century we find Arab physician Al-Razi, also known as Rhazes, codifying the uses of wine distillation and the use of distilled alcohol as a medium for medicinal herbs and berries. During the Moorish occupation of Spain (roughly between 711 and 1492) Arabic scientific and medical knowledge spread across southern Europe through the great monastic houses, then the only centres of learning and knowledge.

In the eleventh century, the Bénédictine monks at the famous medical school of Salerno in Italy used the records of Greek and Arab scholars to create medicines based on combining spirit with various herbs, spices, berries, and roots. The Salerno monks specified the uses of these natural remedies and described them as being made with *aqua ardens* ("burning water" or spirit) in the *Compendium Salerni*, one of the first medical encyclopedias. Sadly they wrote their production methods in code so we have no surviving recipes. But it is almost certain that because juniper grows so rampantly all over Italy, they would have developed a juniper remedy, particularly as the botanical's diuretic effects were already known. It was used widely in the treatment of kidney and bladder diseases. So the most likely candidate as the first producer of a proto-gin appears to be an anonymous monk in the kitchens of a Bénédictine monastery in about 1050.

Arnold de Villa Nova, a thirteenth-century alchemist who taught at the universities of Montpelier and Avignon, was instrumental in spreading the knowledge of distillation. He is credited as the "father of distillation" and wrote, in his *Boke of Wine* of the distillation of wine into *aqua vitae* as well as its subsequent flavouring with various herbs and spices. His description—the "water of life"—has entered every European language: *eau-de-vie* in French, *agua ardente* in Italian, *usquebaugh* in Gaelic (from whence comes the term "whisky").

The re-birth of European distillation took place in the kitchens of mediaeval monasteries and great noble houses. It was almost exclusively concentrated on the manufacture of medicinal cordials and liqueurs. *Aqua vitae* itself was considered to be of great therapeutic value. It was noticed that the rich who drank more freely of it were healthier and lived longer. It took a few more centuries for people to realise that water and milk, the drinks of the poor, were major carriers of disease. *Aqua vitae* itself was taken as a medicine and combined with other botanical ingredients to make life saving elixirs and remedies. Small scale industries grew up, some of whose products still survive—Bénédictine, for example, or Chartreuse (originally, an "elixir of long life", which has been continuously produced since 1605).

In mediaeval Europe a stillatory—a small distillation device—was a standard piece of kitchen equipment and domestic duties included the production of aromatic cordials and liqueurs to be drunk as tonics. Made from a wine spirit, many of them would have included juniper and indeed recipes for juniper cordials survive. A recipe from *Delights for Ladies* gives instructions for one with juniper: "Distill with a gentle heat either in balneo, or ashes, the strong and sweet water wherewith you have drawn oil of cloves, mace, nutmegs, iuniper, rosemarie, &c. after it hath stood one moneth close stopt, and so you shall purchase a delicate spirit of each of the said aromaticall bodies".

Evidence that knowledge of juniper-based medicines had reached the Low Countries came, in 1269, when Flemish poet Jacob van Maerlant te Damme wrote about them in *Der Naturen Bloeme*, a natural history encyclopedia. Later, Antoine de Bourbon, a French aristocrat, invented another proto-gin. Made from a distilled spirit of wine mixed with juniper berries, it became known as "the wine of the poor".

In 1637 the poet Gervase Markham published a guide to household management—*The English Housewife*—in which he indicates a few of the "strong-waters" that a careful housewife should always keep for cases of emergency: "Therefore first I would have her furnish herself of very good stills, for the distillation of all kinds of waters, which stills would either be of tin, or sweet earth, and in them she shall distil all sorts of waters meet for the health of her household, as sage water, which is good for all rheums, and collicks; raddish water, which is good for the stone; angelica water, good against infection; celandine water for sore eyes; vine water, for itchings; rosewater and eye bright water for dimme sights ; rosemary water for fistulaes ; treacle water for mouth cankers ; water of cloves for the pain in the stomach".

DISTILLING WITH GRAIN

As the knowledge of distillation methods became more advanced, it was realised that spirits could be made from any substance that would ferment, not just wine. All over Europe, in the fourteenth and fifteenth centuries, surplus crops were being used to make drinks that were consumed for pleasure: in Poland and Russia potatoes, wheat, and rye were used to make vodka; in Scotland and Ireland whiskies were made from barley.

In the Low Countries, genever's birthplace, *brandewijn* meaning "burnt wine" became the catchall term for all kinds of spirit. Excise records from 1492 indicate that substantial quantities of grain spirit made from local rye were already being produced. In 1582 came the first technical description of grain being used a basis for distilling. In Casper Jansz's *Guide to Distilling Korenbrandewijn* [brandy-wine made from corn] is described as "in aroma and taste almost the same as brandy-wine" and is "not only named brandy-wine but also drunk and paid for as brandy-wine".

GRAIN MEETS JUNIPER

In the early 1500s, numerous records exist of the regulations and taxes imposed on distilleries that were making this new-fangled grain spirit. Many of them were originally farm distilleries as canny farmers found another use for grain they could not sell. *Brandewijn* was fierce stuff and distillers would have experimented with ways to mask its unpleasant flavours. Dr Sylvius de la Böe, who was Professor of Medicine at Leiden University from 1658 to 1672, is often credited as being the first to combine juniper and grain spirit in a medicinal drink called "genever". This is most certainly wrong. For a start, his dates are almost a century out. Secondly, it has become increasingly obvious that no single individual invented genever in the same way that no one person invented vodka or whisky. Medicinal juniper distillates were common throughout Europe at this time and clever distillers quickly realised that juniper and other heavily scented spices combined well with the cheap, locally available brandewijn making it palatable. The fact that the new invention was supposed to be good for you was an extra bonus. Certainly looking at Dutch and Flemish paintings of tavern scenes from this time, one has the distinct impression that people are not drinking genever for its health benefits.

Dutch taverns were frequently depicted in art as places filled with healthy patrons.

Genever production very quickly became industrialised. Between 1500 and 1700, literally hundreds of distilleries sprang up in almost every town all over the Low Countries. In 1602, the Dutch East Indies Company (the famous Vereenigde Oost-Indische Compagnie or VOC) was established and its fleets sailed the Seven Seas, creating the biggest company in the world with—in its heyday—50,000 employees. The sailors and officers on VOC ships received daily half-pint rations of genever in pewter cups. They spread the habit of drinking genever to every port and created a huge trade for their national spirit. In fact, genever is proportionately still the most-exported spirit in commercial history. By 1792, the Dutch were selling 4.2 million gallons of genever abroad annually. Shamefully, as the British were to do later, they used genever as goods in the slave trade. To this day, old stone genever bottles are regularly dug up on remote parts of the coast of West Africa—a reminder of that dark period. In parts of Africa, all spirits are still generically known as "gin" even though most of them bear no resemblance to either genever or gin.

HOW GENEVER IS MADE

Even today, the Dutch call genever "liquid bread". A genever distillery looks very like a huge kitchen with the stills resembling enormous cooking pots: The whole is permeated by a yeasty smell like fresh baked bread.

Dutch genever is made in several stages. First, the "half product" [the base spirit] is made. Nowadays, it can be either a column-distilled molasses or grain spirit, which is then blended with *moutwijn* [maltwine], a grain spirit, made from rye, malted barley and wheat with a fiery taste and a distinctive spirity character. The proportions of half product to maltwine vary according to the style of genever.

Making maltwine—which before the widespread use of the continuous still was the sole spirit used in genever—is still very much a traditional craft akin to making malt whisky. The process starts by pouring a mash of flour and water into giant tubs and adding yeast in order to ferment the liquid. When fermentation is complete, the alcoholic wash is distilled in pot-stills a minimum of three times, each time doubling the alcohol content from 12 percent to 24 percent and then to between 46 percent and 48 percent ABV.

The botanicals used in genever are similar to those used in gin—-juniper, coriander, orange and lemon peels, and angelica—but the recipes often contain stronger, more aromatic ingredients such as St John's wort, caraway, aniseed, hops, and myrrh. As with gin, every recipe is different and there are different methods of adding the botanicals to the base spirit. Sometimes the botanicals are infused in the neutral spirit for several hours and then re-distilled in a pot-still. Or the botanicals can be added to a percentage of the last distillation of maltwine and married with the spirit. Other distillers will combine a percentage of maltwine with a grain or molasses spirit and re-distill the whole with the botanicals. Tradition dictates how different distilleries do it.

There are three styles of genever—oude, jonge, and korenwijn—plus there are aged and unaged varieties. Under EU law each style of genever must contain different minimum percentages of maltwine, botanicals, and sugar as well as be bottled at different alcoholic strengths. This is how it works:

Oude genever is the traditional genever, similar in taste to the original English Genevas. It must contain a minimum of 15 percent maltwine, no more than 20 grammes of sugar per litre and be bottled at least 35 percent ABV. It does not have to be aged but often is. It also often has far higher percentages of maltwine than required. Indeed the original form of *moutwijnjenever* [maltwine genever] usually has around 50 percent maltwine but is now quite rare.

The terms "oude" [old] and "jonge" [young] are confusing as one naturally thinks of aged and unaged. But in this case, they refer to "old style" and "new style".

Jonge genever was developed in the 1950s in response to the demand for a more mixable, lighter-flavoured spirit. It is bottled at a minimum of 35 percent ABV and contains a maximum of 15 percent maltwine and no more than 10 grammes of sugar per litre. If the label mentions "graanjenever" [grain genever], then the base spirit is 100 percent grain. Jonge genever is colourless and very light on the palate.

Korenwijn (or corenwyn) contains a minimum of 51 percent malt-wine so it has a very malty, full-bodied taste. It must be at least 38 percent ABV and contain no more than 20 grammes of sugar per litre. Korenwijn is quite rare outside the Benelux countries but if you come across it, it's definitely worth a try. It's the Dutch equivalent of single malt whisky. Drink it ice cold on its own, or try it mixed in an Old-Fashioned.

GENEVER INVADES

The English first encountered genever during the Thirty Years War (1618–48) when the armies of France, England, and Spain fought over religion, politics, and territory in the Low Countries. Here, English mercenaries were introduced to the local grog, given to steady their nerves before battle. They christened it "Dutch Courage". Later even the great Duke of Marlborough recommended its use "when they were going any time to engage the enemy" and great victories like Blenheim in 1704 and Ramillies in 1706 were credited to its powerful effects. When English soldiers and sailors returned to "blighty" they usually brought their genever habit with them.

However, in 1570, London had become home to 6,000 Flemish Protestant refugees so genever was not unknown in England. Indeed, thousands of gallons of Dutch genever were imported to England in the seventeenth century—legally and illegally —but it was not until the end of the century that the English officially became a nation of spirits drinkers.

GIN'S GLORIOUS REVOLUTION

When the Dutch prince, William of Orange, accepted the invitation to accede to the British throne, in 1688, a complete change in English society—not least in its drinking habits—got underway. William was the son-in-law of the unpopular Stuart king, James II. A Protestant, unlike the hapless Catholic James, William was bitterly opposed to everything Catholic and French. One of his first acts as monarch was to declare war on France. Shortly afterwards, in 1690, legislation was introduced to ban the importation of French wine and brandy and to promote the development of home-grown distilling specifically the production of "good and wholesome brandies, *aqua vitae*, and spirits, drawn and made from malted corn." This was not a purely patriotic gesture, rather it was the result of pressure brought to bear by English landowners who wanted a guaranteed market for their grain in times of surplus. They had been instrumental in supporting William's claim to the throne.

The new legislation opened the doors to a distilling free-for-all. Anyone could distil virtually anywhere once a notice of the intention to distil had been publicly displayed for ten days. The industry consisted of "simple distillers" who, actively encouraged to use English corn (meaning any one of wheat, barley, rye, and oat grains), made a spirit that was usually harsh and unpalatable. It was generically known as "brandy", a copy of the Dutch *brandewijn*. They sold this product to the "compound distillers" who, like the Dutch before them, experimented with different flavours to make it drinkable. Very soon, their attentions turned to genever or geneva, as it was now called. Popular King William and his Dutch court drank it and as a poem in defence of geneva claimed: "Martial William drank Geneva yet no age could ever boast a braver prince than he…". Geneva was fashionable.

In England, spirits had been distilled since Tudor times but the English had never developed large-scale domestic distilling. There are frequent early mentions of *aqua vitae* which, in England, was a crude spirit distilled from fermented grain, fruit, wine dregs or old cider and it had become common practice to carry a supply of spirit in small flasks for use as a restorative. Shakespeare refers to it in many plays notably *The Merry Wives of Windsor*, where a character says: "I will rather trust a Fleming with my butter, Parson Hugh the Welshman with my cheese, an Irishman with my aqua-vitae bottle, or a thief to walk my ambling gelding, than my wife with herself."

In 1621, there were almost 200 small businesses in London and Westminster making *aqua vitae* and "other strong and hott waters" for medicinal purposes. Distilling became regulated when, in 1638, Sir Theodore De Mayerne, a physician and alchemist, founded The Company of Distillers. It received a Royal Charter that gave a monopoly to members of the Company to distill spirits and vinegar in London and within a radius of 21 miles. The Company codified the required methods of distillation and the rules governing its practice. This monopoly and the quality standards that accompanied it were swept away in the Distilling Act of 1690 but returned later. Today the Worshipful Company of Distillers is still one of the City of London's most important institutions engaged in protecting distillers' interests and numerous trade and charitable activities.

Although there were sporadic outbursts of alarm at spirit drinking amongst young men about town, strong water was still mostly medicinal. Samuel Pepys, a renowned social commentator, noted in his famous diary in the entry of 10 October 1663 that: "Sir W. Batten did advise me to take some juniper water.... strong water made of juniper" as a cure for the indigestion that was plaguing him. The fact that Pepys, well known man of fashion and bon viveur, considered these "hot waters" as purely therapeutic is a reliable sign that they had not yet evolved into social drinks. As the century wears on however, we gradually see spirits and what were known as distilled cordial waters, the forerunners of liqueurs, begin to be transformed from medicine into drinks that were drunk for pleasure. After all what worked as a cure for indigestion could then easily be offered as a digestif after a large meal.

THE YEARS OF GIN MADNESS

In 1689, English distillers produced around 500,000 gallons of *aqua vitae* mostly for medical use. Crucial pieces of legislation had continued to further deregulation of distilling, for example, the raising of taxes on beer in 1694 made spirits cheaper than beer for the first time. And, in 1702, the withdrawal of the remaining monopoly of the Distillers Company opened up home grown distilling even further. The 1720 Mutiny Act excused tradesmen who were distillers from having soldiers billeted on them, even more of an encouragement to take up distilling.

Less than fifty years after deregulation, London alone produced 20 million gallons of spirits. This figure did not include the vast quantities of illegal spirit as distillers had developed crafty ways to avoid duties by keeping hidden stills and secret tanks.

The greater part of this spirit went to make what the English now called "geneva". Honest distillers properly redistilled some in the Dutch style but the greater part was cheap corn spirit, usually sweetened, sometimes coloured with prune juice and burnt sugar to resemble brandy, and heavily flavoured with juniper-like substances. It was sometimes stirred into warmed ale and sweetened to make a drink called "purl", but more often mixed two parts water to one part spirit and sold in quarter-pints in one of London's many dram-shops for the price of a penny as "gin".

A whole book could be written about the years of "gin madness" in eighteenth-century London. (Indeed there exists an excellent work, *The Much-Lamented Death of Madam Geneva* by Patrick Dillon, which is devoted to the subject.) By the 1720s, the streets of London were awash with cheap, noxious spirit. The slums of St Giles were a centre for gin drinking as London's poor discovered this new highly addictive drug. This area (behind modern day Oxford Street where Centre Point now stands) was the setting for William Hogarth's famous engraving "Gin Lane"—a visual parable on the shocking effects of the gin mania that gripped the city. Here is pictured the slatternly mother, her legs covered with syphilitic sores, too drunk to notice her child is falling from her arms. Drunkards fight in the street and desperate customers queue at the pawnbrokers in search of money to buy gin. Dangling in the sky is the figure of a bankrupt who has hung himself. Crowds storm Kilman's, the distillers. Carved above the cellar door below is the famous sign: "Drunk for a penny, dead drunk for tuppence, straw for free." Hogarth had been inspired to make this powerful piece of propaganda by statistics such as:

- The death rate in London, in 1723, outstripped the birth rate and remained higher for the next ten years.

- Between 1730 to 1749, 75 percent of all the children christened in London were buried before the age of five.

- At one point, there were 7,044 licensed gin retailers in a city of 600,000 people, plus thousands more street vendors peddling the deadly spirit.

- Between the years 1740 and 1742, in London, there were two burials to every baptism.

- The hospices and hospitals in the City packed with "increasing multitudes of dropsical and consumptive people arising from the effects of spirituous liquors."
- Nine thousand children in London, in 1751, died of alcohol poisoning.

The whole of London society was scandalised by the story of Judith Dufour, who had taken her two-year-old daughter out from the workhouse for the day, strangled her, and sold her clothes to pay for gin. It was extensively reported in the newspapers of the day and contributed to an image of the London poor as a drunken, out-of-control population. Numerous pamphlets and magazine articles denounced gin as the ruin of family life and slowly the demand for reform became unstoppable.

Attempts were made to control the gin madness. They were badly thought out like the one that decreed that only dwelling houses could sell "intoxicating liquors". The Act of 1736 caused the most controversy as it attempted to fix a licence fee of £50 for gin retailers, prohibited the sale of gin in quantities under two gallons and taxed gin at £1 per gallon. The reaction was outrage. This act made Madam Gin the "It Girl" of the summer of 1736, inspiring poetry and pamphlets and even a long-running theatre show written by Henry Fielding, *The Deposing and Death of Queen Gin with the ruin of the Duke of Rum, Marquee de Nantz and the Lord Sugarcane*. Below the Duke of Rum tells how the people reacted to the news that Queen Gin was to be exiled:

RUM:
By different ways their discontent appears:
Some murmur, some lament, some loudly roar,
This day in pomp she takes her leave of all:
Already she has made the tour of Smithfield,
Rag-Fair, Whitechapel and the Clare market: Now
To broad St. Giles she directs her steps.

The play ended with the mob's shout "Liberty, property and Gin forever".

The depictoin of a mock funeral for Madame Geneva on Swallow Street near Piccadilly.

On the actual night before the act became law there was a night of extreme gin madness. Mock funeral processions took place all over the country with people carrying effigies of Madam Geneva. In London, taverns painted their punch bowls and signage black and an official funeral for "Mother Gin" took place in Swallow Street, just off Piccadilly, complete with a horse-drawn funeral carriage and hordes of mourners dressed in black, drinking the last legal gin in copious quantities.

Nothing much changed. In fact, sales of illicit gin— now sardonically called "Parliamentary Brandy'"—soared, and in 1742 the Act was repealed.

THE GIN OF THE GIN CRAZE

The only thing that modern gin has in common with the gin of the "Gin Craze" is their shared name: And even that started out as derogatory term as the upper classes' sarcastic description of this new opium of the masses. However gin was a word enthusiastically adopted by its devotees although it had many other nicknames—Madam Geneva, Ladies Delight, Royal Poverty, My Lady's Eye-water, Kill-Grief, Cock-my-Cap, King Theodore of Corsica, and Blue Lightning (because habitual gin-drinkers faces often turned blue), to name just a few.

What were London's slum dwellers drinking and just why was it so detrimental to their health? A recipe from the actually quite respectable firm of Beaufoy, James, and Co in Vauxhall gives some idea:

- Oil of vitriol (sulphuric acid): Gave poorly rectified spirit an extra kick and made it go further.
- Oil of almonds: A cheap flavouring substituted for the coriander and other spices used in Dutch genever.
- Oil of turpentine: Used because its piney, resin flavour mimicked the flavour of juniper berries but was much cheaper.
- Spirits of wine: The base spirit, probably not a wine spirit as the first distillation of grain was called "low wines".
- Lump sugar: Blended in to disguise the off flavours.
- Lime water: Employed for flavour.
- Rose water: Incorporated for bouquet.
- Alum: Used to make the spirit taste better.
- Salt of tartar: Added as another way to improve the taste of the spirit.

Juniper and other botanicals are conspicuous by their absence. But this distiller was following a quite common practice. It is estimated that, in 1735, approximately five million gallons of gin were made from similar recipes. An interesting footnote here is that Mark Beaufoy, a partner in the business, apparently turned his back on the distilling trade after seeing Hogarth's "Gin Lane" illustration.

In London's slums much worse gin was drunk. The traditional way of purifying spirit by re-distillation was expensive, time consuming, and required skill—not to mention proper pot-stills and distillation equipment. Setting up a distillery could cost as much as £4,000—a staggering sum in those days. The bootleg-distillers in St Giles and the East End needed much quicker results. So sulphuric acid, rock salt, and quick lime were used to purify cheap spirit or "low wine" [that is, spirit] that had been distilled once or at the most twice. They threw in anything else that was lying around and, according to the anti-gin crusaders, that often included rotten fruit, urine, and animal bones. They stirred in pepper, ginger, plus other hot ingredients to make the spirit taste stronger and more authentic. Almost certainly they sneaked in hard maltum, a preparation made from *cocculus indicus*, a poisonous alkaloid more commonly employed as a pesticide, which had stupefying effects and was frequently used by nefarious brewers to make beer more inebriating.

At the same time, however, there were reputable distillers plying their craft, making proper geneva and hollands—direct copies of the Dutch prototype. Ambrose Cooper's 1757 book, *The Complete Distiller*, was the distiller's bible. One of the most fascinating things found in this manual is the insight it gives into the vast range of natural flavourings then available. Ordinary folk relied on natural remedies to cure all manner of ills and Cooper's manual details every conceivable type of fruit, flower, seed, berry, and herb that could be used to make "waters" and "cordials" for therapeutic use. He describes the properties of the various plants, what they can heal, when they should be picked and how they should best be stored. His handbook gives numerous recipes and instructions for different drinks including one for geneva described thus: "There was formerly kept in the apothecaries shops a distilled spirituous Water of Juniper but the Vulgar being fond of it as a dram, the distillers supplanted the apothecaries and sold it under the name of Geneva. The common sort is not made from juniper berries as it ought to be but from Oil of Turpentine".

Ambrose's recipe is quite different: "for making 10 gallons of Geneva—take of juniper berries three pounds, proof spirit 10 gallons [proof was then equivalent to 51 percent ABV] water 4 gallons. Draw off by a gentle fire until the feints begin to rise and make up your goods to the strength required with clean water. The Distillers generally call those goods which are made up proof by the name of Royal Geneva; for the common sort is much below proof, ten gallons of spirit being sufficient for fifteen gallons of Geneva".

Geneva was expensive and consumed by the upper classes. Ambrose then goes on to give a description of "what is sold at the alehouses", similar to the recipe of Beaufoy and James. He comments wryly: "it is surprising that people should accustom themselves to drinking it for pleasure." He also gives an important clue to the difference between geneva and hollands. It's long been assumed that they are different names for the same spirit but not according to Ambrose. He says the recipe for hollands is the same as the one for "royal geneva" but that the distiller "may make a Geneva equal to the Dutch provided it be kept to a proper age." So geneva is unaged, hollands is aged.

AN INDUSTRY IS BORN

In 1743 the Government introduced yet another gin act. This one achieved a balance between the need to control gin production, urgent now given that spirit production had reached 8 million gallons with only around 40 gallons declared for duty, and pragmatism. Licences of £1 to sell gin were given to those who already held beer and ale licences and distillers were not allowed to retail gin direct to the public but only to licensed houses. Rather than trying to enforce a form of prohibition, the British Parliament encouraged proper controls and moderation, far more realistic goals.

Spurred on by the success of this act and a rising anti-gin crusade, Parliament passed a law in 1751, known as the Tippling Act. Only established licensed public houses could now sell gin. If credit was given to customers, sums under £1 were not recoverable in law and those in charge of jails and workhouses were specifically forbidden to retail alcohol.

By further controlling those who could sell gin and by raising excise duties to a level that would discourage the back street boys, the Tippling Act dragged gin kicking and screaming out of the gutter. Taxes and duties on gin began to produce a valuable source of revenue for the public purse and the excise duty on spirits was raised steadily—from £7 7s 0d in 1751 to £61 19s 9d in 1791. Prices rose correspondingly and consumption fell. During the years of bad harvest between 1757 and 1760, the distillation of spirits from corn was prohibited. This had such beneficial effects on the health of the common people, that Parliament was inundated with demands that the prohibition should be permanent.

The farmers protested vociferously. A compromise was reached and the duty was raised yet again.

By the closing stages of the eighteenth century The Gin Craze was over. Ever increasing excise duties meant gin was no longer cheap, no longer the drug of the poor. Stricter controls like the specification of the minimum size of a still led to the proper supervision and management of distillation. It drove out the unscrupulous. Capital was now required to invest in a proper distillery. This encouraged respectable companies to begin to make quality products and it is no coincidence that the rise of the great English distilling houses dates from this time.

London was the centre of the trade and, by 1790, was producing 90 percent of English gin. As the English city with the biggest population there was never-ending demand. There were also very practical reasons why London became so important to the distilling industry. From its earliest times, the growth and prosperity of London was based on the fact that it had an estuary with a double tide that allowed goods to be brought up the River Thames from the sea into the heart of the city. By the time reputable gin distilling had developed in the late eighteenth century, London's dockyards had doubled in size and expanded eastwards. Then London was the biggest and busiest port in the world. Tourists came from all over Europe to gaze at the Pool of London and marvel at how it was possible to walk from one side of the river to the other on the mass of ships that were moored there.

Thanks to the River Thames, the motorway of its time, London's distillers had easy access to the raw ingredients they needed: oranges, lemons, spices and herbs brought in by the East India Company; sugar from British colonies in the Caribbean; grain brought in from East Anglia and Kent.

In 1794, there were around 40 distillers, malt distillers, and rectifiers, in the cities of London and Westminster, and Southwark, according to one contemporary trade directory. Compare this with 50 years earlier when there were reckoned to be 1,500 in the same area with most owning less than £100 worth of equipment.

LONDON'S DISTILLERS

One of the most important things to realise about early nineteenth-century distillers is that they did not just make a single product as modern distillers do. Surviving price lists and recipes confirm that all of the major distillers made an enormous range of alcoholic drinks, many of which were still regarded as restorative tonics. Like James Burrough of Beefeater, who described himself as distiller of "foreign liqueurs" and distilled anything that could be distilled: liqueurs and cordials from imported French brandy combined with natural flavourings; fruit gins such as blackcurrant, raspberry, sloe, orange, ginger, lovage, and lemon; plus bitters, shrubs, punches, geneva, Old Tom gin, and eventually dry gin. There are even references to the pick-me-up qualities of a magical brew called "coca wine"!

By this time, the industry had developed into a small number of large malt distillers who produced the primary spirit, which they then sold to a much larger number of smaller distillers, who re-distilled it into products sold under their own names. This may have been because the excise duty was higher on the primary alcohol. The primary distillers were often based in east London and, in the period between 1802 and 1820, they were responsible for between 70 and 80 percent of all the spirit charged with duty in England. They tended to be major concerns often involved in brewing and pig farming as well with the pigs being fed the waste products of the brewing and distilling processes, a rather forward-looking eco approach.

Distilling had become big business with a number of London trades-people dependent on it for their living. A contemporary account describes them as "coopers, backmakers, coppersmiths, wormmakers, smiths, bricklayers, plumbers, all concerned in the coal trade, all employed on the land producing the corn, landlords, those that carry it to the sea or waterside, captains and masters, sailors, bargemen, corn factors, millers, and all those involved in bringing in spices, seeds, and sugar from abroad." Farmers, too, relied on the distilling trade as it allowed them to sell surplus- and below-standard grain at a profit. It is estimated that, in the 1820s, around three-quarters of the grain sold in the London corn market was sold to distillers.

Because large quantities of clean water are required in the distillation process, many distillers were located in those parts of London that were not only convenient for river transport but also close to sources of pure water. Clerkenwell, the site of an ancient and sacred spring called Clerk's Well, was a distilling hub. It was connected directly to the docks via the River Fleet, then the second largest river in London. Booth's was in Clerkenwell probably from around 1740 and had a substantial distillery there by 1778. Nicholson's, once a great name in English distilling, had a large distillery in Clerkenwell. Alexander Gordon moved his business, in 1786, from Southwark to Clerkenwell. Later, in 1832, Charles Tanqueray set up his distillery close to a source of pure spa water further west in Bloomsbury. And James Burrough of Beefeater Gin acquired the Taylor distillery in Chelsea in 1863.

The introduction of a minimum legal still capacity led to smaller firms, who did not have the resources to invest in production, being swallowed up by larger ones. Gradually the industry became concentrated into fewer hands. Distilling was a profitable business. It had shaken off its disreputable image and distillers continued to grow in importance and prestige. A major sign of recognition for the trade came when one of their number, Sir Robert Burnett, was made Sheriff of the City of London in 1794. And, as the ever waspish Boswell comments in his *Life of Johnson*: "Foreigners are not a little amazed when they hear of brewers, distillers and men in similar departments of trade held forth as persons of considerable consequence".

Now we find firms like Gordon's sourcing their base spirit from grain whisky producers in Scotland and an increasing emphasis on quality methods of production and quality ingredients. The Haigs and the Steins, who dominated the legal distilling industry in Scotland, first dabbled in the gin trade in 1777, exporting 2000 gallons of grain spirit to London. By 1782 this had risen to 184,000 gallons. Legislation of 1823 had transformed Scottish distilling by halving duties and permitting volume production of a better quality of spirit. Licensed production of malt and grain spirit increased greatly and much of this soon found its way south of the Border for rectification into gin despite screams of protest from English primary distillers.

Around this time too gin was no longer seen as the drink of the poor and desperate. The sporting men about town of Regency London were fond of it. There's a witty description of gin drinking in the various strata of London society in a very popular imitation of London journalist Pierce Egan's famous *Life in London*. Published in 1821 it was known as *The Real Life of London" - The Rambles and Adventures of Bob Tallyho, Esq. and His Cousin, the Hon. Tom Dashall, through the Metropolis; Exhibiting a Living Picture of Fashionable Characters, Manners, and Amusements in High and Low Life. By an Amateur.*

At this time gin had many nicknames—daffy, blue ruin, Old Tom, max, flash of lightning, and jackey, amongst others. Tom Dashall talks about them all in detail:

"Daffy's Elixir," replied Dashall, "was a celebrated quack medicine, formerly sold by a celebrated Doctor of that name, and recommended by him as a cure for all diseases incident to the human frame. Gin, Old Tom, and Blue Ruin, are equally recommended in the present day; in consequence of which, some of the learned gentlemen of the sporting world have given it the title of Daffy's, though this excellent beverage is known by many other names.

"For instance, the Lady of refined sentiments and delicate nerves, feels the necessity of a little cordial refreshment, to brighten the one and enliven the other, and therefore takes it on the sly, under the polite appellation of white wine. The knowing Kids and dashing Swells are for a drap of blue ruin, to keep all things in good twig. The Laundress, who disdains to be termed a dry washer dearly loves a dollop of Old Tom, because, while she is up to her elbows in suds, and surrounded with steam, she thinks a drap of the old gemman (having no pretensions to a young one) would comfort and strengthen her inside, and consequently swallows the inspiring dram. The travelling Cat-gut Scraper, and the Hurdy-Grinder think there is music in the sound of max, and can toss off their kevartern to any tune in good time. The Painter considers it desirable to produce effect by mingling his dead white with a little sky blue. The Donkey driver and the Fish-fag are bang-up for a flash of lightning, to illumine their ideas. The Cyprian, whose marchings and counter marchings in search of custom are productive of extreme fatigue, may, in some degree, be said to owe her existence to Jackey; at least she considers him a dear boy, and deserving her best attentions, so long as she has any power. The Link-boys, the Mud-larks, and the Watermen, who hang round public-house doors to feed horses, &c. club up their brads for a kevartern of Stark-naked in three outs. The Sempstress and Straw Bonnet-maker are for a yard of White Tape; and the Swell Covies and Out and Outers, find nothing so refreshing after a night's spree, when the victualling-office is out of order, as a little Fuller's-earth, or a dose of Daffy's; so that it may fairly be presumed it is a universal beverage--nay, so much so, that a certain gentleman of City notoriety, though he has not yet obtained a seat in St. Stephen's Chapel, with an ingenuity equal to that of the Bug-destroyer to the King has latterly decorated his house, not a hundred miles from Cripplegate, with the words Wine and Brandy Merchant to Her Majesty, in large letters, from which circumstance his depository of the refreshing and invigorating articles of life has obtained the appellation of the Queen's Gin Shop."

(A kevarten is a quartern or dram of gin and a Cyprian is a prostitute)

THE RECTIFIERS' CLUB

One reason why the distillation industry grew so rapidly in prestige and influence was that London's distillers joined forces to protect their mutual interests. The Rectifiers' Club was formed, in 1820, and lasted until the late 1840s. Over time, the list of members included all the great names of the London distilling industry, including many that survived until well into the twentieth century and even some that are still around today.

The Rectifiers met once a month in the London Tavern for dinner. According to the club records, held in the Guildhall Library, in 1837 Mr Gordon placed half a dozen bottles of champagne on the table to celebrate the engagement of his daughter to Mr Edward Tanqueray. Within this bonhomie and socialising, a lot of hard business was accomplished: for example, agreeing to fix the prices of gin, bitters, cordials and liqueurs amongst themselves. As is the way of these things, the next meeting recorded complaints that some members were underselling contrary to the agreement. Rises in the price of spirits, due to ever increasing taxation, were a common subject of debate. The Rectifiers wrote a joint letter, in March of 1825, to the Chancellor of the Exchequer, asking him to bring forward his proposed reduction of duty on spirit as they "are suffering a great stagnation of sales" and want "a revival in demand." Amazingly, the Chancellor agreed.

It seems clear that London's distillers were a very tight-knit group, many related to each other, marrying into each other's families and very able to act as one to defend the interest of their trade. One could almost describe them as a mafia.

OLD TOM GIN

At the beginning of the nineteenth century, the gin sold in barrels to retailers was often accompanied by descriptors such as "Old Tom", "Young Tom", "Celebrated Cream Gin", "Cream of the Valley", and "Out and Out". What seemed to have happened over time was that, in much the same way, as the word "Hoover" became the common name for any type of vacuum cleaner, Old Tom became the generic name for gin and later evolved into the term distillers used for sweetened gin. In the beginning, however, all gin was sweetened: First, because sugar very effectively masked fusel oil flavours in the base spirit before the invention of the continuous still allowed a clean neutral spirit to be made; secondly, because popular taste leant toward sweetness. Old Tom was then produced around 25 percent ABV and was sold in drams in the gin palaces to be drunk neat like a liqueur.

In taste terms, Old Tom gin is often described as the missing link between Dutch genever and modern dry gin. It's not quite as simple as that. Having encountered a bottle of London-distilled Old Tom gin from about 1890 in the offices of Master Distiller Desmond Payne it was interesting to discover that it tasted more like juniper-flavoured new-make whisky than genever, albeit with a distinct sweetness. As with all gin the quality of Old Tom gin would have varied greatly then as there were not the rigorous controls there are today over the quality of the spirit.

Each distiller would have had his own recipe too. Some Old Toms would have been like a liqueur—heavily sweetened with sugar and glycerine as well as strongly flavoured with juniper and other herbs—often described as "cordial gin". But most distillers simply added sugar to their recipes for Old Tom gin. An original 1864 recipe for dry and Old Tom gin found in the Beefeater Distillery lists juniper berries, coriander seed, angelica root, ground liquorice root, and winter savoury as the botanical recipe for both dry and Old Tom gins. This is a valuable document as it strongly indicates that many distillers used the same botanicals for both types of gin but added sugar to the Old Tom version—in this case the proportions are specified as 40 pounds of loaf sugar for every 100 gallons of spirit. A few distillers didn't use sugar at all but instead employed botanicals like liquorice and sweet fennel to achieve a musky sweetness.

As distilling techniques advanced, the quality of the spirit dramatically improved but this sweetened gin was still popular so distillers continued to make it and, in fact, charge more for it than for Dry Gin.

It is believed that Old Tom gin got its name from a certain Captain Dudley Bradstreet, an enterprising bootlegger. When the first spectacularly unsuccessful attempt to control gin sales was made in 1736, he acquired a property on Blue Anchor Lane and invested £13 in gin purchased from Langdale's distillery in Holborn. He set up a painted wooden sign of a cat in the window and broadcast the fact that gin could be purchased "by the cat". Under the cat's paw sign there was a slot and a lead pipe, which was attached to a funnel situated inside the house. Customers placed their money in the slot and duly received their gin. Bradstreet's business prospered until complaints about the "cat-man" became too numerous and competitors emerged. His idea was soon copied all over St Giles where people would stand outside houses, call out "puss" and when the voice within replied "mew", they knew that they could buy bootleg gin inside. By the middle of the eighteenth century, Old Tom was the street name for gin.

There are other stories too like the one of the cat that fell into the barrel of gin immortalised in Boord's famous Cat and Barrel trademark of 1849 for Old Tom gin, the first ever patent for gin. However Joseph Boord offered a different story for the product's origin, claiming under oath in a famous trademark dispute case that his gin was named for an "Old Tom" who worked at another distillery.

Another popular theory posits this man as Thomas Chamberlain at Hodges' distillery in Lambeth. His apprentice Tom Norris, opened a gin palace in Great Russell Street, Covent Garden where he sold gin from casks purchased from his former employers as "Old Tom". The only problem with this theory is that the dates don't quite match.

There are numerous literary and other references to Old Tom gin from 1800 onwards particularly notably in the drawings of Thomas Rowlandson. a famous Regency satirist. So unlikely as it seems the story of the bold Captain Bradstreet might have some truth and what is certainly true is that by the time branded bottles came in, most brands of Old Tom gin carried an illustration of a black cat.

Old Tom gin remained fashionable until the turn of the century and many cocktail recipes from this period specify it in such drinks as the Martinez and the Tom Collins. In fact, many cocktail books right up until the 1950s, such as David Embury's 1948 *The Fine Art of Mixing Drinks*, claim that a Tom Collins can only be made with Old Tom gin.

Old Tom and dry gin existed side by side until the turn of the century but then gradually dry gin began to edge out Old Tom because the taste for very sweet drinks waned. Old Tom gin continued to be made in Plymouth and Warrington and by all the major London firms until around the 1960s when, because of lack of demand, production slowly ceased. Old Tom then became virtually extinct but it's become available again as a number of Old Tom-style gins have launched in response to modern bartenders' desire to create the authentic cocktails of yester year. (see the chapter titled Gin Brands for details)

THE RISE OF LONDON DRY

Throughout the early nineteenth century, when people drank gin, they usually drank Old Tom, Geneva or Hollands. But by the 1850s, something else happened too, and that was the gradual displacement of heavy, sweet gin by unsweetened, clear gin. It came to be known as the London dry style. "Dry" because it was unsweetened—or as distillers liked to advertise it—"sugar free gin." "London" because most of the distillers making it were based in London.

There are several reasons why this new style of gin gradually took over. First, of course, was the widespread use of the continuous still that allowed a purer, more consistent spirit to be cost-effectively made. Now the quality of a pure grain spirit could be enhanced with more subtle flavours rather than disguised with sugar and heavy aromatics. Secondly, a great disaster overtook London's distillers in the 1870s, when the impact of the dreaded phylloxera blight was felt. Phylloxera was an aphid infestation imported on vine stock shipped from the USA to France in 1862, which destroyed most of Europe's vineyards. Consequently, brandy became almost unobtainable.

Let's not forget that all distillers then still made a huge variety of liqueurs using French brandy. Cherry brandy, curaçaos, parfait amour, ginger brandy, maraschino, noyeau, and others were the big sellers. Suddenly an entire income stream disappeared. Distillers realised that they had to diversify. Many of them began to bottle Scotch and Irish whiskies as "British liqueurs". They also began to look at gin with new eyes as the upper classes, now deprived of brandy, drank gin in greater quantities and wanted a more sophisticated spirit. One only has to look at the stock lists of distillers like Beefeater's founder James Burrough to see that, from 1876, there was an increasing emphasis on gin, now sold under brand names such as Ye Old Chelsey, Black Cat Gin, James Burrough London Dry and Old Tom Gins, and even an aged Fine Old Malt Gin. Other distillers took the same route, not least because slowly but surely gin was crawling out of the back streets to become a drink for the affluent middle classes.

Despite another minor gin panic in the 1830s, attitudes toward drink and drinking fundamentally changed during Queen Victoria's long reign. Throughout the eighteenth century one thing those at the top of the social scale and those at the bottom had had in common was a love of excessive drinking. In 1773 Dr Johnson spoke of a time when "all the decent people in Lichfield got drunk every night and were not thought the worse of." By Victoria's time drunkenness was not socially acceptable amongst the upper classes and the lower classes were to be actively saved from the evils of drink.

The British Temperance movement started in Preston in Lancashire in 1832 with the signing of the first abstinence pledge. Many thousands signed the oath at mass rallies. Influential people joined the cause, believing that the working class needed to be protected from themselves. But the prohibitionists never had much real political success in Britain however. Their achievement was to lobby for and drive through legislation to control when, how, and by whom alcohol could be sold, much of which was beneficial. Who, for example, could argue with outlawing the practice of selling small children "squibs"—the child-size portions of gin sold by unscrupulous landlords?

Ironically the failure of the prohibitionists to completely ban the sale and consumption of alcohol, enshrined the right to drink in British law, which was encapsulated by the bishop who roundly declared during yet another stormy licensing debate in the House of Lords: "I would rather see England free than England sober".

Later when the Liberal government sought re-election in 1874, it was rejected by voters, bitter about Gladstone's capitulations to prohibitionism: "We have been borne down in a torrent of gin,..." the defeated Gladstone wrote.

Spirits were still seen as the problem: drinking beer was perceived as wholesome and somehow English. Even the original Temperancers had no beef with ale or beer. One should never forget that the companion piece to Hogarth's illustration "Gin Lane" was "Beer Town". In "Beer Town" (reputedly sponsored by a cartel of London brewers) all was quiet, orderly, and peaceful. As part of the anti-gin drive, the consumption of beer was actively encouraged. By 1836, there were 56,000 licensed beer shops in England and Wales. Many were dirty and ramshackle so magistrates demanded improvements before granting and renewing licences. Beer shop owners often borrowed money from the major brewers in order to make the necessary improvements. In return they promised to only buy supplies from the brewers who funded them. This "tied house" system was to have a major effect on gin's rise to respectability.

Gin shops were forced to compete with these new upmarket pubs and so transformed themselves into gin palaces. The arrival of these gin palaces introduced the idea of drinking as a social activity, part of daily life, not merely a shortcut to oblivion. The first to open in London was probably that of Thompson & Fearon's in Holborn in around 1832. Whilst many disapproved, the gin palaces—especially in contrast to the dingy gin shops of old—were the last word in luxury and glamour, a place where ordinary people could escape the drudgery of work and the meanness of their surroundings. Soon these were a feature of life in industrial cities. (In fact many fine examples remain despite the vandalism of the 1970s: The Barley Mow, The Princess Louise, and The Salisbury in London; The Café Royal in Edinburgh; The Horseshoe in Glasgow; and perhaps one of the most famous bars in the world—The Crown in Belfast which is now owned by the National Trust who spent over £400,000 to restore it to its original palatial glory.)

Dickens describes gin palaces in *Sketches by Boz* in Hemingway-esque terms:

"You turn the corner. What a change. All is light and brilliancy. The hum of many voices issues from that splendid gin-shop which forms the commencement of the two streets opposite; and the gay building with the fantastically ornamented parapet, the illuminated clock, the plate-glass windows surrounded by stucco rosettes, and its profusion of gas-lights in richly-gilt burners, is perfectly dazzling when contrasted with the dirt and dark we have just left. The interior is even gayer than the exterior. A bar of French-polished mahogany, elegantly-carved, extends the whole width of the place; and there are two side-aisles of great casks, painted green and gold, and bearing such inscriptions as 'Old Tom, 549'; 'Young Tom, 360'; 'Samson, 1421' the figures agreeing, we presume, with 'gallons' understand. Beyond the bar is a lofty and spacious saloon, full of the same enticing vessels, with a gallery running round it, equally well furnished. On the counter, in addition to the usual spirit apparatus, are two or three little baskets of cakes and biscuits which are carefully secured at the top with wicker-work to prevent their contents being unlawfully extracted".

ONWARDS AND UPWARDS

Until the mid nineteenth century all UK produced gin was for the domestic market. Heavy excise duties handicapped the export trade until, in 1850, Sir Felix Booth of the London distilling family spent a small fortune on pushing a private bill through Parliament to remove excise duties on export gin. Gin soon became an important export, earning money for the Treasury and boosting Britain's worldwide reputation as the source of everything excellent. The trade was kick started by the Royal Navy. In the early nineteenth century, gin Was the drink of officers on Navy ships. Wherever the Navy went, gin went too. (The connection between gin and the Navy remains in the "gin pennant," the green-and-white flag traditionally run up as an invitation to board for drinks.) Requests for London and Plymouth gins poured in from every corner of the world with Gordon's, for example, sending a shipment to a group of Australian miners who paid in gold dust.

This was also the great age of colonialisation when the sun never set on the British Empire. For thousands of expats serving in far-flung outposts English gin was not just a cure for homesickness, it was a life-saver, literally. They drank it with another new invention—Indian tonic water—to prevent malaria. When they finally came home to the Home Counties, they brought the taste for this new, sophisticated drink with them.

Genteel Victorian women bought the new-style gin in grocery shops thanks to a law of 1861 that allowed the stores to retail spirits. They served gin at tea parties from decanters labelled "Nig" in a bourgeois attempt to confuse the servants. By this time, the fashion for "banting" or slimming was in full swing and people had begun to realise the danger of indulging in sugar and starch. Tastes changed, veering away from sweet to more subtle flavours and "sugar-free" was the epitome of quality.

English distillers began to sell gin, in the 1880s, in proprietary bottles to cater for the off-licence trade. Up until then gin had been sold in barrels and the retailers poured it into containers for their customers to take home. The first gin bottles were dark green and heart shaped—straight copies of Dutch genever bottles. Later bottles were made of clear glass because export customers wanted to see exactly what they had purchased. (Domestic Gordon's Gin is still sold in dark green bottles and export gin in clear, a throwback to this practice). Soon sophisticated packaging and advertising promoted London dry Gin as a quality product.

In 1898 Gordon's and Tanqueray joined forces to become the major presence in the English distilling industry. Their combined economic power was enormous. Through rationalisation of their production processes and the beginnings of a marketing strategy, they positioned gin as a truly sophisticated international drink.

GIN COMES INTO ITS OWN

One reason for the new dry gin's ultimate success is that it was more mixable than the heavier sweet style. It worked far better in the new craze for cocktails, which had first arrived in Europe in the 1860s, brought over by Americans who imported the fashion for sweet mixed drinks.

The debate on the etymology of the cocktail rages still with drinks historians undecided as to the definitive answer on the word's origin. This theory proposed by the great American humourist and author HL Mencken in his 1948 article *The Vocabulary of the Drinking Chamber* somehow seems to have more plausibility than most and it's entertaining:

"I have in my archives perhaps forty or fifty such etymologies for cocktail, but can only report sadly that all of them are no more than baloney. The most plausible that I have encountered was launched upon humanity by Stanley Clisby Arthur, author of *Famous New Orleans Drinks and How to Mix Them*, a classical work. It is to the effect that the cocktails was invented, along about 1800, by Antoine Amédée Peychaud, a refugee from Santo Domingo who operated a New Orleans pharmacy in the Rue Royale. This Peychaud was a Freemason, and his brethren in the craft took to dropping in at his drugstore after their lodge meetings. A hospitable fellow, he regaled them with a toddy made of French brandy, sugar, water, and a bitters of a secret formula, brought from Santo Domingo. Apparently running short of toddy glasses, he served this mixture in double-ended eggcups, called, in French "*coquetiers*". The true pronunciation of the word was something on the order of "ko-kayt-yay" but his American friends soon mangled it to "cock-tay" and then to cocktail. The composition of the bitters he used remained secret, and they are known as Peychaud's to this day"

Wealthy refugees from the French Caribbean colony of Santo Domingo who fled after the slave uprisings of the 1790s played an important role in sophisticating New Orleans so the idea that the widespread use of the word "cocktail" originated in this place at this time is believable.

However, more recently, historians Jareed Brown and Anistatia Miller discovered the use of the word "cocktail" in an item that appeared on 20 March 1798. London's *Morning Post and Gazetteer* satirically listed details of 17 politicians' pub debts, including the following:

Mr Pitt,
two petit vers of "L'huile de Venus"   0 1 0
Ditto, one of "perfeit amour"   0 0 7
Ditto, "cock-tail" (vulgarly called ginger) 0 0 3/4

The fact that the "cock-tail" was one of Mr Pitt's drinks—listed after two obviously French beverages—suggests that the word "cock-tail" might have had French origins. After all, Mr Pitt's tenure as Premier (as the Prime Minister was called back then) was marked by the French Revolution and the Napoleonic Wars.

Even though the word was used in Britain before it was found in the States, cocktails became closely associated with Americans for one reason. American-style cocktails differed from Victorian drinks such as cups, punches, toddies, flips, fizzes, daisies, cobblers and slings, in that they were heavily iced. The establishment of the Wenham Lake Ice Company on the Strand in 1845 made ice commercially available in London for the first time. The first American cocktail bar opened in the 1860s, behind the Bank of England and soon cocktail bars popped up all over London. The Criterion in Piccadilly opened in 1870 and grand hotels like the Savoy and Claridge's boasted the inclusion of American bars with a wide range of cocktails based on gin. Some Londoners disapproved.

In 1863, Henry Porter and George Roberts expressed their opinion in print: "for the sensation drinks which have lately travelled across the Atlantic we have no friendly feeling ...we will pass the American Bar... and express our gratification at the slight success which 'Pick-me-up', and 'Corpse Reviver' have had in this country". However Mrs Isabella Beeton, the domestic goddess of Victorian England, begged to disagree and included recipes for Mint Juleps and Gin Slings in her famous 1861 *Book of Household Management*.

Cocktails caught on and cocktail books featuring gin recipes were widely published. Jerry "the Professor" Thomas's 1862 *The Bar-Tender's Guide and Bon Vivant's Companion* appeared. He toured Europe, in 1859, with his own travelling bar giving demonstrations and many European bartenders came to learn from the master. Harry Johnson's 1882 book, *Bartender's Manual or How to Mix Drinks of the Present Style* was another bestseller.

In the United States, imported English dry gin and Old Tom gin were sold in equal amounts until the 1890s. But from then on dry gin became the preferred cocktail spirit. There, the Dry Martini and the Bronx—both dry gin drinks—were the most popular cocktails.

PROHIBITION

On January 17th 1920, the Volstead Act passed through the US Congress. Prohibition came into force. It soon turned into a re-enactment of the eighteenth-century Gin Craze as millions of ordinary Americans turned into amateur distillers and professional drinkers. A popular song summed up the mood:

Mother makes brandy from cherries
Pop distils whisky and gin;
Sister sells wine from the grapes on our vine—
Good grief how the money rolls in

Organised crime quickly moved in on illicit alcohol manufacture and smuggling as there were vast profits to be made. An entire generation of Americans became criminals in one form or another either by going to speakeasies to drink, distilling at home or buying bootleg booze. Not exactly the scenario envisaged when many US towns closed down their jails on the eve of Prohibition in the anticipation that, once alcohol was banned, there would be no more crime.

Bathtub gin was popular. It was a vile combination of industrial alcohol, glycerine, and juniper oil made in large containers to which water was added via the bath tap. To make it taste better people added fruit juices, mixers, and bitters inventing a raft of new cocktails.

English distillers feared losing their most important export market as a result of Prohibition. In fact, the reputation of imported English gin reached new heights as, having experienced the effects of truly bad alcohol, people were ready to pay exorbitant sums for the real stuff. It is estimated that during Prohibition London distilleries exported around 40 million dollars worth of gin to the US via Canada, the West Indies, and islands close to American shores. No questions were asked when requests came in that orders should be packaged so that they could float.

On the 5th December 1933, the "noble experiment" ended, brought to a close largely by the very people who had been the most vociferous in support of the ban. American mothers, weary of seeing their families become official criminals and the obscene profits made by gangsters like Al Capone and Dutch Schultz, led the charge to repeal the act. Franklin D Roosevelt had run for President on a platform that included ending Prohibition. It is rumoured that he mixed the first legal Martini that night in the White House for thirteen years using Plymouth Gin.

America re-entered the civilised world: The reputation and prestige of English gin had never been higher.

DRY GIN RULES SUPREME

The 1920s and 1930s were gin's glory days. It was the age of glamour, an explosion of the new in technology, music, fashion, the arts, and popular culture. Along with fast cars, short skirts, bobbed hair, modern art, cinema, and jazz, drinking cocktails was the height of fashion.

London of the 1920s saw the arrival of many of America's leading barmen and cocktail experts who had come in search of work, driven from home by Prohibition. By now gin cocktails were simpler and new, sophisticated drinks such as the Clover Club and the White Lady were lapped up by high society in cocktail bars like Ciro's Club, presided over by legendary Scottish bartender Harry MacElhone, and the American Bar at the Savoy.

The writer Evelyn Waugh described the racy lives of young moneyed aristocrats in novels, christening them the "Bright Young Things". Newspapers and magazines were fascinated by everything this smart set did, the first glimmerings of the modern obsession with celebrity. They were a distraction from the economic depression and mass unemployment of the years between the two World Wars, a time when the old formal social order began to disappear. Cocktail parties became the rage, copying the American fashion of replacing the British custom of afternoon tea with early evening cocktails in grand hotels. Dressing up for formal dinners Was abandoned and the cocktail hour was the perfect way to fill the vacuum, creating another opportunity for frantic socialising.

In his novel *Vile Bodies*, Waugh describes the constant frantic social whirl: "Masked parties, savage parties, Victorian parties, Greek parties, Russian parties, circus parties, parties where one had to dress as somebody else, almost naked parties in St John's Wood, parties in flats and studios and houses and ships and hotels and nightclubs, in windmills and swimming baths ... all the succession and repetition of massed humanity. ... Those vile bodies." There was even a baby party, with cocktails served in nursery mugs.

Gin was the spur for this manic pace of life. In Noël Coward's 1926 stage play *Words and Music*, the chorus of debutantes sings:

> *"The Gin is lasting out*
> *No matter whose*
> *We're merely casting out*
> *The Blues.*
> *For Gin in Cruel*
> *Sober Truth*
> *Supplies the Fuel*
> *For Flaming Youth"*.

Riding the cocktail zeitgeist, distillers became much more sophisticated in their marketing. "Drinks never taste thin with Gordon's Gin" was the strapline for Gordon's advertising. At this time, Plymouth Gin and Booth's Gin were the two most famous gin brands in the world and both invested heavily in promoting their products. Booth's Gin published *An Anthology of Cocktails* in the 1930s, which featured the favourite cocktails of society figures, and heart throbs such as silent-screen idol Ivor Novello.

Further down the social scale gin was "in", too. Cocktails never invaded the pub where the most popular mixers for gin were bitters, orange squash, ginger beer, peppermint and lime cordials as well as tonic water. A perennial favourite in working men's pubs was the Dog's Nose—a glass of gin poured into a pint of beer.

During the Second World War, all distilling from grain was prohibited to conserve stocks of grain for food. Most distilled alcohol was diverted to the war effort: described by the stoical British as "Cocktails for Hitler". However, despite strict rationing, some gin was still made for the domestic market using a molasses spirit. Once the war was over, English distillers were back in action, building huge export trades and making imported English-made gin the world's most sophisticated spirit.

The popularity of gin reached its apogee in the '50s and '60s with Hollywood stars such as Errol Flynn and Humphrey Bogart rarely seen without a Gin Martini in hand. Gin was glamorous: to this day the last take of every Hollywood movie is still called the "Martini shot" as that was the signal for everyone, from big name star to the guy who holds the clapper board, to celebrate in style with a Gin Martini.

Gin was sophisticated and the three-Martini lunch, which US President Jimmy Carter later condemned, was standard fare in sophisticated New York circles. David Embury's *The Fine Art of Mixing Drinks* published in 1948, made cocktail making at home seem easy. Very few middle-class American households did not have their own cocktail bar where mixing a Martini was the evening ritual.

Gin remained the dominant white spirit right up until the early 1960s, a time when probably around half of any cocktail list would be made up of gin based drinks. Then came vodka. By the 1970s, gin was almost stagnant in terms of growth. Many traditional brands simply disappeared. Others sat unloved on dusty shelves with no investment and no innovation. Even worse, gin lost its iconic image and was perceived as the opposite of "cool"—a drink your parents drank.

Times change. Gin is once more the star of the scene. Its revival can be dated back to 1988, when Bombay Sapphire launched. Stylish packaging and a less juniper-dominated taste profile attracted a whole new audience for gin. Bombay Sapphire proved it was possible to re-invent the category. Its success was the catalyst for a wave of activity and a host of new, unusually-flavoured gins have emerged and are still emerging.

The 1990s cocktail renaissance also put gin firmly back in the spotlight. No two gins taste quite the same. High-quality gins with interesting new flavours inspire bartenders to come up with drinks that showcase gin's unique personality as well as different brands' specific botanical recipes. At the same time, there's been a revival of interest in the traditional brands and classic cocktails. Gin, a spirit with flavour, heritage and provenance, is now back—big time.

GIN BRANDS

The brands reviewed here are alphabetically arranged. With very few exceptions they are all premium gins, bottled at above 40 percent ABV. Or they are brands with an interesting history. This is by no means a comprehensive list and although UK made gins dominate, the best American, French, and Spanish gins are also included. All are widely available either in retail or on the web.

AVIATION

In the USA, microdistilling, like microbrewing before it, has taken off. There are currently around 90 craft distilleries. In 1990, there were five. American microdistillers have tapped into the backlash against mass-produced products and experiment with a range of premium small-batch spirits. Increasingly, it's gin. Reinventing the London dry formula, they push exotic citrus and aromatic ingredients to the forefront and let juniper take a back seat. Aviation Gin is typical of this style. It's a collaboration between House Spirits Distilling in Portland, Oregon and mixologist Ryan Magarian, made with the Aviation cocktail in mind. Botanicals in the mix are juniper, cardamom, coriander, lavender, anise seed, sarsaparilla, and dried orange peel. Re-distilled with a 100 percent rye-grain neutral spirit and bottled at 42 percent ABV there are strong hints of Dutch jonge genever. Aviation is the ideal base for the many citrus-based vintage gin cocktails that are back in fashion again.

BEEFEATER DRY

James Burrough, the founder of Beefeater Gin, was born in Devon in 1835. He trained as a pharmacist in Exeter before setting off to seek his fortune in North America. Five years later James returned to the UK in search of his next commercial opportunity. That was the Chelsea distilling and rectifying firm of John Taylor, established in 1820, which James purchased, in 1863, for £400.

Taylor specialised in the production of liqueurs, fruit gins, gin, and punches. The distillery had an excellent reputation and loyal customers such as Fortnum & Mason. James took over the business renaming it "James Burrough, Distiller and Importer of Foreign Liqueurs". He used his knowledge of science to perfect his recipes. The business did well and, in 1871, James began to improve and extend the distillery buildings.

When the phylloxera blight struck European vineyards, James turned his attention to the domestic spirit that would benefit enormously from the ensuing brandy shortage—English gin. A notebook, from 1879, shows that James constantly experimented with different proportions of orange in his gin recipe, perhaps because he had found a reliable supplier in Covent Garden and the orange-based liqueurs were his most successful.

Beefeater is an exceptionally clean, bold gin whose extravagant juniper character is balanced with very strong citrus. On the nose, juniper is dominant whilst in the mouth the full-bodied aromatic character of the gin emerges, to be followed by a long and complex finish. Still made to

James Burrough's original recipe, it contains juniper, coriander, Seville orange peel, lemon peel, almond, angelica root and seed plus liquorice, Beefeater owes its distinctively clean taste to the fact that it is based on a pure grain spirit. Another reason for Beefeater's rich character could be the fact that it is made by the steeping method, where the botanicals are steeped in the grain spirit for 24 hours before being gently heated and allowed to run through the still. The final spirit is reduced to 40 percent ABV.

Beefeater is the only London dry gin from the glory days when London-made gin dominated, that is still made in London at its distillery in Kennington—a cricket ball's throw away from the famous Oval cricketing ground. Beefeater has always had a major export trade thanks to its early positioning as a characteristically "English" product. That tradition continues: Beefeater is still a leading brand in over 170 countries around the world.

BEEFEATER 24

Beefeater 24 is the luxury super-premium addition to the Beefeater Gin portfolio launched in October 2008. Like Beefeater Dry, Beefeater 24 is made in the heart of London. Like Dry, it's also made by the steeping method.

Master Distiller Desmond Payne has applied his years of experience to the creation of 24. Having long been fascinated by the potential of tea in the botanicals mix, he was delighted to discover that the father of James Burrough had been a tea merchant in London, supplying fine teas by Royal Appointment to Queen Victoria. Building on this historic link, Payne's voyage of discovery began. After almost two years of constant experimentation, the recipe was complete. It includes the core botanicals that define the distinctive, instantly recognisable Beefeater taste—juniper, coriander, angelica root and seed, almond, Seville orange peel, lemon peel, orris plus liquorice. To these are added a unique blend of Chinese green and rare Japanese sencha teas plus a citrus boost in the form of grapefruit peel. The spirit is "cut" at an earlier stage and a smaller percentage of the run is taken in order to retain the fresher, more volatile flavours of grapefruit and the leaf teas.

On the nose, notes of citrus, juniper and the aromatic scent of sencha are immediately apparent. In the mouth, there's a burst of citrus followed by juniper developing into a long finish with spicy coriander balanced by the dryness of angelica and the woodiness of liquorice. Beefeater 24 is a London dry Gin, which means that no colouring or flavour has been added after distillation. Bottled at 45 percent ABV, it's a glamorous, sophisticated spirit that has inspired some of the world's top mixologists to come up with stunning new cocktails.

BERKELEY SQUARE

Berkeley Square is a premium gin from master distillers G & J Greenall that is inspired by the herbs of an English physic garden. To the core botanicals of juniper, coriander, angelica, and cubebs is added basil, sage, lavender, and citrus in the form of kaffir lime leaves. It is made in a two-day process using a bouquet garni technique. First, the core botanicals and the kaffir lime leaves are placed in a copper pot-still filled with triple-distilled grain spirit, which is left to macerate for a day. The other botanicals are then wrapped in muslin and steeped in the spirit to infuse their oils. On the second day, the still is run very slowly and gently to pick up the delicate essential oils of the bouquet garni.

Whilst it's not at its best in a G & T, the green herbaceous botanicals in Berkeley Square make it an ideal gin to experiment with for interesting herbal cocktails.

BLOOM GIN

Another relative newbie from the G & J Greenall stable in Warrington, Bloom is aimed squarely at the female market. It's based on a triple-distilled pure grain spirit and uses honeysuckle, pomelo, and chamomile in addition to the more "standard" botanicals. The idea here is to recreate the classic aromas of an English country garden and there is no doubt that Bloom is on the light, fresh, and floral side of the flavour spectrum. Honeysuckle provides an aromatic sweetness like candied fruit whilst the essential oils of pomelo (a close relation of grapefruit) adds another citrus dimension

BLUECOAT GIN

Named after the blue uniforms of the American militia in the Revolution, this gin—made in Philadelphia, PA—describes itself as an American dry gin, a far better name than the attempts to designate new style US gins as "New Western Dry". The differentiating feature of Bluecoat is the use of organic juniper and citrus in a neutral grain spirit made from rye, wheat, barley, and corn that is then filtered before bottling at 47 percent ABV. Batch distilled over a long, slow ten-hour process the resulting liquid is exceptionally smooth with juniper and citrus notes and traces of rose hip and grapefruit.

BOMBAY ORIGINAL DRY GIN

Bombay Original Dry has been around since the late 1950s, launched by American Alan Subin. He saw the opportunity to create a new gin to challenge Tanqueray and Beefeater in the United States and approached the Greenalls Distillery in Warrington with a name and a marketing plan, but without a specific taste. Greenalls came up with Bombay Dry based on a gin recipe found in their archives dating back to the 1760s. Based on a 100 percent pure grain spirit and bottled at 40 percent ABV, it's a London dry gin that uses eight botanicals—the traditional ones plus almonds, liquorice, and cassia bark. Like its younger sister it's made by vapour distillation in a Carterhead still.

On the nose juniper, coriander and liquorice dominate. The taste is full-bodied with piney juniper, lemony citrus, and warm spice. Initially Bombay Dry was distilled at Warrington and bottled in Edinburgh. In 1964 it was bottled at source. Bacardi Martini now owns all Bombay brands. For far too long, Bombay Original was only widely available in Spain and the United States, the decision has been taken to extend distribution to the UK and other European territories. Which is good news for gin fans. Equally good news in 2012 was The Bombay Spirit Company's unveiling of plans to build a new distillery and visitor centre in Hampshire, a short distance from London, and move all gin production there.

BOMBAY SAPPHIRE

Bombay Sapphire is the gin that gently led the category out of its dog days. Developed in the 1980s by Michel Roux, the driving force behind Absolut Vodka, it's a lighter juniper premium gin that has attracted a whole new audience to the category. Using the Bombay Original Dry recipe as the starting point, Sapphire adds a spicier coriander, cubeb berries, and West African grains of paradise. It is made in a Carterhead still picking up these more subtle spicy and fragrant aromas. Stylish packaging and a distinctive blue bottle make Bombay Sapphire instantly recognisable on every back bar. Its success has encouraged other gin distillers to experiment with innovative ingredients. Perhaps the biggest favour Bombay Sapphire has done for gin, however, is that it was the first brand to actually talk about what's inside the bottle. That got bartenders exploring different botanical flavours and Dick Bradsell's famous Bramble is believed to have been inspired by Bombay Sapphire.

Bombay Sapphire tends to be more laid back than many other London dry gins. On tasting it's slightly sweet on the nose with delicate juniper, spice, and citrus flavours following on. Fresh and clean with an elegant finish Bombay Sapphire is a barkeep's dream with extraordinary versatility in long drinks and cocktails. Speciality Sapphire serves include the Aviation made with crème de violette and the Wet Martini where the extra vermouth enhances Sapphire's floral and spice flavours.

BOMBAY SAPPHIRE EAST

A new variant of the classic Bombay recipe, Bombay Sapphire East adds Thai lemongrass and Vietnamese black peppercorns to juniper, citrus, angelica, orris root, coriander, liquorice, cassia bark, almonds, cubeb berries, and West African grains of paradise. Where Bombay Sapphire is characterised by delicate juniper, spice, and lemon flavours, Bombay Sapphire East makes its presence felt with a lovely big pepper hit. Fragrant spice and a citrus sweetness combine to add complexity and weight. Bombay Sapphire East is very much aimed at the G & T market, where these spicy, earthy flavours more than hold their own against even the sweetest of tonic water.

BOOTH'S GIN

A document of 1569 refers to the Booth family's involvement in the wine trade. Once can presume that they expanded into gin distilling as many wine merchants did, although there is no official record until the listing of Philip Booth & Company Distillers in Clerkenwell in the 1778 Directory of Merchants. This makes Booth's and its sister brand Boord's among the oldest gin brands still in existence.

In 1819 Philip's son, Felix Booth, gained control of the business and built another distillery in Brentford on a quay by the Thames. Felix rapidly transformed Booth's into the largest distiller in the country. He was a philanthropist. In 1829, Booth anonymously funded Captain John Ross' expedition to map the elusive North West Passage. The mission did not succeed in this but did find the true position of the magnetic North Pole. In his wanderings around the Arctic, no doubt sustained by copious amounts of Booth's Gin, Ross named many of the areas he mapped after his patron. That's why you still bizarrely find Boothia Peninsula, Felix Harbour, Cape Felix, and the Gulf of Boothia in northern Canada. Booth also, at great personal cost, successfully lobbied for legislation to allow gin to be bottled in bond for export thus opening up the international gin export trade.

In the following century, Sir Felix Booth expanded the business and turned it into the largest distilling company in England. The family owned Booth's until 1896 when, on the death of the last male Booth, it became a limited company. During the 1920s and '30s Booth's expanded and diversified, acquiring more than twelve different spirits companies including Boord's, an equally venerable brand. Booth's became the premium English gin. The company made several London dry style gins: Booth's Finest, High & Dry, and House of Lords. To promote them Booth's published *An Anthology of Cocktails* in the 1930s, which featured the cocktail choices and photographs of society figures and well-known characters such as Ivor Novello and Lady Oxford. It was an instant hit, both for cocktails and Booth's Gin.

Booth's Finest was distinguished by its very slightly golden colour, the result of being aged in sherry casks. Unfortunately in later years, when advertising and marketing for gin began to focus on cleanness and purity, the reputation of this slightly coloured gin suffered. After the war the company targeted Booth's High & Dry, a very light, dry gin ideal for cocktails, at the American market in order to compete with Tanqueray. It never quite managed and Booth's gins went into a slow but steady decline from which they never fully recovered.

The Booth and Boord brands are now owned by Diageo Spirits. Booth's gins are no longer made in the UK, but are available in the US where sadly they have become very much bottom shelf brands. For a long time Boord's continued to be made in the UK exclusively for Pimms No 1, a not totally undignified fate for a once great brand.

BOUDIER SAFFRON GIN

In the eighteenth and nineteenth centuries, there was a substantial gin industry in northern France which, let's not forget, was once part of the Low Countries and hence genever heartland. Saffron Gin, made by famous micro-distillers, Gabriel Boudier of Dijon, is a reminder of this history. Based on a nineteenth-century colonial recipe, Saffron Gin is rich in the exotic botanicals that were the fashion at that time—juniper, coriander, lemon, orange peel, angelica seeds, iris, fennel, and of course, saffron. Deep orange in colour, it's heavily infused with saffron and has a subtle spiciness derived from fennel plus angelica seed. The ideal drinking occasion is as an apéritif served with tonic and a slice of orange to enhance the colour and flavour where it adds a whole new dimension of Campari-like herbal bitterness.

BROKER'S GIN

Brothers Martin and Andy Dawson created Broker's Gin in the late 1990s. It's a very English brand with its bowler hat and typical old-fashioned city gent pinstripe livery.

Broker's is batch-distilled in a copper pot-still made by John Dore, the Rolls Royce of still-makers, at the Langley Distillery. The botanical mix of juniper berries, coriander seeds, cassia bark, cinnamon, liquorice, orris, nutmeg, orange peel, lemon peel, and angelica root is first steeped for 24 hours in triple-distilled neutral grain spirit made from 100 percent English wheat. It's a classic London Dry Gin with a rich aromatic nose and an intense flavour and makes no bones about it. The recipe is 200 years old, so all the botanicals are conventional gin botanicals: no off the wall ingredients. And its owners created it for people who really like gin and appreciate a big juniper hit. Spirits guru F Paul Pacult sums up the taste experience: "In the mouth it sits well on the tongue and, thankfully, is the proper level of alcohol for gin, 94 proof. It finishes long, semi-sweet, tangy and luscious. A superbly made London dry gin that deserves a very close look by any admirer of that style."

BULLDOG

Although Bulldog Gin is owned by a former investment banker based in New York, it's a very classic London dry gin distilled in London and made from 100 percent British grain. Quadruple distilled and triple filtered for extra smoothness, Bulldog is made with unusually exotic botanicals that include lotus leaves, lavender, poppy, and the reputedly aphrodisiac Dragon Eye, a cousin of the lychee fruit. It also has a distinctive look with a very butch smoked-grey tinted bottle and spiked collar. Big, bold flavours and a refreshingly crisp character make this one for a Martini especially the dirty version.

BURNETT'S WHITE SATIN

Burnett's White Satin is a venerable English brand that was established by Robert Burnett in the late eighteenth century. He acquired a huge distillery in Vauxhall that had been built by in 1767 by Sir Joseph Mawbey. It was then the biggest distillery in London. Contemporary reports of the time record that there were seldom less than 2,000 hogs constantly grunting, and kept entirely on the grains. (A common practice of distillers at the time was to keep pigs and feed them on the waste from distilling—very eco). Robert Burnett became Sheriff of London, in 1794, and was knighted the following year.

Burnett's White Satin is another classic English brand that has experienced a rollercoaster ride. For years, it was one of the biggest selling gins in the UK but was then demoted to a cheap compounded gin made with molasses spirit and artificial flavourings. Recently, however, it has returned to its roots as a traditionally distilled proper London dry gin made with grain spirit and natural botanicals. Crisp and clean on the nose it has warm spicy flavours, and a fresh, juniper palate.

CADENHEAD'S OLD RAJ

Cadenhead's Old Raj gin is actually neither a London or a Distilled gin and is technically made by cold compounding. The reason it's included here is because, despite that, it's a damn fine gin, probably because of its exceptionally high strength. Old Raj is made by steeping each botanical in a mixture of alcohol and water, then distilling them separately in a small pot-still. The resulting essences are then combined with a neutral grain spirit and saffron is added for colouring. At 46 percent abv, it is spirity and peppery with a slight medicinal taste from the high alcohol content. At 55 percent it is very aromatic, full and rounded.

CAORUNN GIN

Scottish whisky distillers are at the forefront of the great gin revival. No wonder – they have the stills, the spirit and generations of distilling expertise. Caorunn (pronounced "ka-roon") Gin is small batch gin made in Scotland by Inver House Distillers, the malt whisky experts at the Balmenach Distillery on Speyside.

Caorunn is Gaelic for the rowanberry. This gin includes rowanberries and a further ten botanicals: six traditional ones plus some unusual, particularly Scottish ingredients such as Coul Blush apple, heather, bog myrtle, and dandelion. It is made by a unique vapour infusion method where an exceptionally pure neutral grain spirit is heated to vapour in a special still called a Copper Berry Chamber, made in the 1920s.

The chamber is round and contains four large trays on which the botanicals are placed. As the vapour passes through the trays it picks up the flavours of the botanicals in a long slow process. When it cools and returns to liquid the botanicals are firmly embedded in the spirit.

Reduced with pure, soft Scottish water to a bottling strength of 41.8 percent ABV, Caorunn is a real taste adventure. On the nose it's juniper with fruity notes of rowan and apple that develops beautifully into a clean, crisp, aromatic flavours with a pronounced fruitiness and slight heather honey sweetness. A long dry finish makes this one for those who are fans of mellow gins. In its striking bottle, five sided to represent the five botanicals in the blend with graphics influenced by the Scottish Art Nouveau movement, Caorunn is already inspiring bartenders to come up with new and unusual cocktails to make the most of its distinctive flavours.

CASCADE MOUNTAIN GIN

Cascade Mountain Gin is made in the wilds of Oregon at the small Ben Distillery. Its major point of difference is that it uses locally grown, wild juniper berries that are hand picked alongside other northwestern botanicals. The natural juniper gives this gin a very slight straw colour, which is not filtered out. Juniper dominates and at 95 proof Cascade Mountain Gin is not to be messed with.

CITADELLE GIN

Citadelle Gin is made in Ars, France, by Cognac's Gabriel & Andreu according to a 1771 recipe that was created by the Citadelle Distillery in Dunkirk—the old genever heartland. It has 19 botanicals including such rarities as savory, fennel, violets, and star anise. The use of so many botanicals somewhat stifles the juniper but does give this gin unusual aromatic, herbal notes, and a pleasantly perfumed palate. A new Citadelle Réserve has been launched in a limited edition. Aged for six months in oak, it has a fuller juniper taste with a slight oakiness. Both are bottled at 44 percent ABV or 88 proof.

CORK DRY GIN

Cork Dry Gin was first made at the Old Watercourse Distillery— established near Cork, Ireland in 1793—according to an original recipe, using spices and herbs brought to the port of Cork. Now it's made at the Middleton Distilleries by Irish Distillers and bottled at 38 percent ABV, which is not nearly as good as the export version produced at 43 percent ABV. Cork Dry is triple distilled and is sweeter than many UK-produced dry gins as a result of the use of sweeter citrus, reputedly tangerine. It is not a big juniper gin, but has sherberty, mellow flavours that make it a good everyday gin. It's Ireland's biggest seller.

DARNLEY'S VIEW GIN

When the Wemyss family, renowned for their expertise in fine wines and spirits, were thinking of a name for their new gin they didn't have to look far. Their historic family home Wemyss Castle in Scotland was the place where Mary Queen of Scots first spied her future husband, Lord Darnley, in 1565. Bottled at 40 percent ABV Darnley's View is clean and fresh on the nose with the aromas of very distinctive juniper. In the mouth juniper develops strongly complemented by sharp lemon citrus and mellow spice with laid back floral notes. The finish is long and dry. Darnley's View is the ideal summer gin and works very well in summery drinks like an Elderflower Collins and a Gin Fizz.

In 2012 sister gin Darnley's View Spiced Gin was launched. In this recipe the elderflower has been dropped. Spiced Gin contains juniper, cinnamon, nutmeg, cassia, grains of paradise, ginger, cumin, cloves, coriander seed, and angelica root. Jason Scott of the world famous Bramble Bar in Edinburgh has worked with the company to to create some stunning new drinks such as a Spiced Ginger Martini, Spiced Gin East India Daisy—a new recommended serve with ginger ale—and a Hot Spiced Gin Punch to complement the warm winter flavours of the new addition. It works very well with citrus-laden drinks and goes perfectly with proprietary Bitter Lemon, a mixer that should be seen much more nowadays.

DEATH'S DOOR GIN

Another offering from the flourishing US micro-distilling scene, this one comes from a small distillery based on Washington Island in Wisconsin. Death's Door Spirits works with local farmers to grow organic and sustainable grains. It has become a leading force in craft distilling. Bottled at a hefty 47 percent ABV, Death's Door Gin is made from a mix of local organic hard red winter wheat and organic malted barley. Unusually, it is distilled at their own distillery and then redistilled with only three botanicals—juniper, coriander, and fennel. The juniper grows wild on Washington Island while the coriander and fennel come from mainland Wisconsin. Not surprisingly, given this minimalist approach it's dominated on the nose by juniper aromas quickly followed by celery and coriander notes. Interestingly as the taste develops in the mouth fruit and sweet spice come to the fore.

DH KRAHN GIN

This relatively new US gin sits firmly in the London style in terms of taste, but is not produced like a traditional London gin. It is made by macerating botanicals and then re-distilling them with neutral spirit in a patented Stupfler pot-still. The gin is then left to age slightly in steel barrels so no colour is picked up. The recipe is simple with only six botanicals: Italian juniper, Moroccan coriander seed, Floridian oranges, Californian lemon and grapefruit as well as a touch of Thai ginger. The Thai ginger is an inspired ingredient, adding an almost chilli tang to the sweet fruit and citrus profile. Ideal in a Martini.

EDINBURGH GIN

The Spencerfield Spirit Company developed Edinburgh Gin inspired by the discovery that Edinburgh and its port—the Port of Leith—were once great centres of gin distilling. When gin became the fashionable spirit in the nineteenth century, Edinburgh distillers, like their London counterparts, produced gin—originally a direct copy of Dutch genever—to cater for demand. Like the London distillers they had everything they needed arriving on the quays of the Port of Leith, then one of the biggest ports in northern Europe

Edinburgh Gin is a small batch, big juniper gin with a peculiarly Scottish twist. It starts life south of the Border in the Black Country in a revered 200-year-old Scottish copper pot-still in which Scottish grain spirit is distilled together with the classic gin botanicals, such as juniper, coriander, citrus peel, angelica, and orris in the traditional way. It is then shipped to Scotland where a carefully chosen selection of distinctively Scottish botanicals in the form of softer, less pungent Scottish juniper as well as heather and milk thistle are added. Finally it is bottled in Scotland at a hefty 43 percent ABV.

On the nose it's clean, fresh and spicy. On tasting, pine comes to the forefront with heathery scented notes following. A well-balanced crisp gin with a gingery spiciness and laid back citrus.

EDGERTON PINK GIN

For purists there's something inherently wrong in the concept of a pink gin. But strangely Edgerton works, mainly because one expects it to be sweet and it isn't. At 47 percent ABV it also packs a massive very non girly punch. The pinkness reputedly derives from the pomegranate. Edgerton also contains sweet orange peel, cassia bark, nutmeg, grains of paradise, and damiana—a Mexican plant that provides a hint of mint.

At the Thames Distillery in London these are steeped together with the more usual gin botanicals for 24 hours before they are distilled in pure grain spirit. Edgerton Pink has crisp citrus top notes balanced by the spice flavours of the more aromatic botanicals.

FIFTY POUNDS

Crafted at Thames Distillers in London, Fifty Pounds Gin takes its name from the unsuccessful 1736 Gin Act when a £50 tax was levied on those wishing to produce and sell gin. Only two distilleries ever agreed to pay it.

It has eleven botanicals including eight of the classics but the remaining three are part of the secret recipe. Unusually after distillation the spirit is rested for three weeks to allow the flavor of the botanicals to fully develop. Bottled at 43.5 percent ABV, Fifty Pounds Gin's big traditional flavours have made it a hit with gin aficionados all over the world. On the nose there's massive juniper, lemon zest, and sage aromas. In the mouth, there's a bit of sweetness and a juniper, orange and lemon citrus led palate whilst fresh minty notes emerge in the finish.

FOXDENTON ESTATE 48 GIN

Foxdenton 48 is a small batch gin made at Thames Distillers in London. The brand is owned by Nicholas Radclyffe, the sixth generation of his family to own and manage the Foxdenton estate in Buckinghamshire. It's a classic London dry that has been developed specifically for the G&T. A simple recipe, it has six botanicals: juniper, coriander, angelica, orris, lemon peel, and lime flower oil. Big on juniper with a refreshing citrus kick and floral hints from the lime flowers, it delivers everything a classic English gin should. The Foxdenton Company also makes a range of excellent fruit gins—sloe, raspberry, plum, and damson.

GILBEY'S SPECIAL DRY GIN

Established by brothers Walter and Alfred Gilbey, in 1857, on their return from service in the Crimean War, the Gilbey's empire eventually expanded to include a substantial wine and whisky business plus a large number of off-licence shops. But it was gin that made the Gilbey's name. In 1872, the brothers began to produce their own gin at their Camden Town Distillery. Earlier they had purchased the landmark Pantheon building in Oxford Street as offices.

Gilbey's Gin soon became the leading brand in British colonies. By the 1920s, distilleries were built in Australia and Canada. During Prohibition, regular consignments of Gilbey's Gin were shipped to Antwerp and Hamburg. From there they travelled to just outside the 12-mile limit of the US coastline and then smuggled into the States. In fact, so in demand was Gilbey's during Prohibition that it was widely counterfeited. The company introduced a special frosted bottle that was difficult to copy.

Now owned by Diageo, Gilbey's is no longer made in the UK and rarely seen there. It's produced in Australia, Canada, New Zealand, South Africa, and the USA. It remains a huge brand in commonwealth countries.

GIN MARE

Produced in a fishing village on Spain's Costa Dorado, Gin Mare bills itself as the "gin of the Mediterranean" using botanicals sourced within the Mediterranean area. Thus the traditional botanicals—juniper, bitter orange peel, Seville orange peel, lemon peel, cardamom, and coriander—are enhanced by the more unusual olives, basil, rosemary and thyme. Production is unconventional too with all the botanicals, save the citrus ones, macerated individually for 24 to 36 hours in neutral grain alcohol, then individually distilled in a copper pot-still. The citrus botanicals are macerated in neutral grain alcohol for 300 days and then distilled. Finally, all the botanicals are blended together and bottled at 42.7 percent ABV.

The result is a different kind of gin: more fiery and schnapps like with juniper very evident. The Mediterranean botanicals come through strongly giving interesting herbal, savoury notes enhanced by the pungency of rosemary.

GORDON'S SPECIAL DRY GIN

Alexander Gordon was born in London on 10 August 1742. His father, George Gordon, was a native of Aberdeen, who allegedly left Scotland due to his involvement in the 1715 Jacobite uprising. Alexander founded his distillery in Southwark, in 1769, and then moved it, in 1786, to Clerkenwell. He had ten children, one of whom, Charles, carried on the family business when Alexander died as an honoured citizen of London. His son, another Charles, sold the firm, in 1878, to John Currie & Co Distillers from the Four Mills Distillery at Bromley by Bow.Currie & Co had provided Gordon's with spirit for rectification for many years. Tanqueray already had a close commercial relationship with the Curries and, in 1898, Gordon and Tanqueray combined to create Tanqueray, Gordon & Co. This move established the two companies as the most powerful force in English distilling, a position they still hold.

Today Gordon's is the number two selling global gin (only outsold by the vile Ginebra San Miguel made in the Philippines) with distilleries in the UK, the USA, Canada, South America, and Jamaica.

Gordon's is a very traditional London gin made to the original recipe which specifies ginger, cassia oil, and nutmeg as well as the more commonly found juniper and coriander. Sold in the UK at 37.5 percent ABV it is very juniper and lemony with a clean sharp aftertaste that works well in a Gin & Tonic, which is how it's mostly drunk.

But Gordon's Export Strength at 47.3 percent ABV is a whole different ball game—more flavourful and more aromatic. A very interesting version—Gordon's Distiller's Cut—made with ginger and lemongrass was launched a few years ago. It was rashly discontinued which is a great pity. But it's still out there and worth tracking down if you can find it.

GREENALL'S ORIGINAL LONDON DRY

G & J Greenall has been producing gin since 1761, the year that Thomas Dakin built a distillery in the centre of Warrington, then a great centre for brewing and distilling. In 1870, Edward Greenall, a member of an established Lancashire brewing family, bought the Dakin Company and acquired ownership of a successful business with an established distribution network.

In the mid-1960s, a new distillery, bottling facilities, and warehouses were built on land close to the site of the original distillery. This allowed Greenall to expand into contract distilling. Disaster struck, in 2005, when the entire premises was almost destroyed by fire. But the distillery was saved and was able to continue to make a number of prestigious gins including Bombay Sapphire.

Greenall's Original Gin contains eight different botanicals, including the less-common cassia bark and ground almonds. It is distilled four times and made according to a 1761 recipe in a still that was built in 1831. It is bottled at 40 percent ABV (80 proof) and is strongly citrus on the nose, developing into dry rounded juniper notes. G & J Greenall Bloom is a recent arrival to the portfolio. It's a much more delicate, summery gin made with botanicals such as chamomile, pomelo, lavender, and honeysuckle with a light, floral taste and strong violet notes. The company also makes a range of canned gin drinks and has huge markets in eastern Europe, particularly in Russia, where people are regularly spotted downing them on the way to work in the morning.

G'VINE

G'Vine gins are the brainchild of EuroWineGate, the French company who make Ciroc, the first vodka made from grapes. The gins are produced from Ugni Blanc grapes that are distilled four times to create a grape neutral spirit. The base of G'Vine Floraison is unique as it consists of the rare vine flower, which blooms for a few days in June (this blossoming period is known in France as the *"floraison"*, hence the name). The flowers are immediately macerated in the grape neutral spirit for two to five days and then distilled in a small copper Florentine still. Meanwhile nine botanicals—ginger root, liquorice, green cardamom, cassia bark, coriander, juniper berries, cubeb berries, nutmeg, and lime—are infused in separate families (juniper berries, then spices, then aromatics) in the grape neutral spirit for several days before distillation in small copper pot-stills. Finally, the vine flower infusion, the three botanical distillates, and more grape spirit are blended and copper-pot distilled one final time.

A new version, G'Vine Nouaison, named for the berry on the vine that grows into a grape, has increased juniper and nutmeg components, less vine flower and is bottled at a higher 43.9 percent ABV. Whilst G'Vine gins may not be for the juniper enthusiast, their light, floaty, floral flavours come to the fore in citrus-based drink especially when lime is in the mix.

HAYMAN'S GINS

Christopher Hayman inherited his passion for gin distilling from his great grandfather James Burrough who created Beefeater Gin in the 1800s. The Haymans are the oldest English distilling family still involved in the trade. Rather like their illustrious ancestor, Hayman's Distillers make several different types of gin. Hayman's London Dry Gin is a fine example of the classic handcrafted London style. The mix of ten botanicals is steeped with triple-distilled neutral grain spirit in a traditional pot-still for 24 hours before distilling begins. The result is a crisp and elegant gin in which juniper, coriander and strong citrus elements are carefully balanced.

The company has also led the revival of Old Tom gin. Hayman's Old Tom is distilled from an original family recipe from the 1870s. It's distilled in the traditional way with more pungent botanicals like nutmeg, cassia bark, cinnamon, and liquorice layered on a juniper and citrus profile which is sweetened with sugar. It's an authentic recreation of the Old Tom style once made by most English distillers with one crucial difference in that the spirit is properly rectified. It's much sought after by bartenders who want to experiment with original cocktail recipes from the glory days.

Hayman's 1820 Gin Liqueur is similar to the cordial gins of bygone days. It's made from 100 percent pure grain spirit with a subtle blend of botanicals with aromatic juniper and fruity notes. It's best served neat, on the rocks.

HENDRICK'S GIN

Some years ago, when whisky experts William S Grant & Sons decided to apply their distilling expertise to the production of a new gin, the brief was to come up with a super premium that would be lighter and less juniper dominated than other gins on the market. The traditional tastes of English summer were to be the starting point. For months, the team worked in the lab, endlessly experimenting with different botanicals in the quest to get the right balance. It's not easy, as even minute quantities of a particular ingredient can alter the entire taste spectrum. After much trial and error, they arrived at the final botanicals—juniper, orris root, angelica, coriander, lemon and orange peel, caraway seeds, chamomile flowers, elderflowers, cubeb berries, and meadowsweet with a final infusion of distilled oils of cucumber and Bulgarian *rosa damascena* [Damascus rose].

Having developed an unusual recipe, it's not surprising that William S Grant should adopt a different approach to making their new baby. Hendrick's is small-batch distilled using two different methods—pot-still and infusion. In the former, a quantity of botanicals and neutral grain spirit are placed in the distillery's Bennett pot-still, dating from the 1860s, where it is gently "boiled" in the traditional way. A specially adapted Carterhead still, one of only four in the world, is used for the infusion method. Think of the different results you get when you steam vegetables. That is the effect—cleaner, subtler flavours. The two distillates are combined and then cucumber plus rose distillates added.

The percentage of pot distilled to infusion distilled is part of the secret recipe. But the combination of the strong, aromatic flavours achieved in a pot-still with the more subtle, volatile flavours picked up in the Carterhead are obvious in the final taste of Hendrick's. It results in fresh, floral, slightly aromatic notes, combined with silky smooth texture and mouth-feel. Hendrick's is one of the gins that has led the renewed interest in gin and works particularly well in drinks like the Elderflower Collins and the Elderflower Martini.

ISH GIN

Ish Gin is the brainchild of two fully-paid-up gin devotees Ellie Baker and Fran Ameijeiras, husband and wife owners of the Bristol Bar in Madrid, who have one of the largest range of gins in the gin crazy Spanish capital. It contains eleven botanicals with a surprising twist in the form of extra juniper—that is, double the amount of juniper normally employed. It's made in London and is a London dry gin. After distillation the concentrate is allowed to rest for two weeks before it is blended with more natural grain spirit and then reduced to the desired alcoholic strength of 41 percent ABV with water.

On tasting, the extra juniper makes its presence strongly felt and there are also hints of spice and lime in a well-balanced botanicals profile.

JENSEN'S BERMONDSEY GINS

Jensen's Bermondsey Gin is the brainchild of Christian Jensen, a Danish IT specialist who fell in love with old-style gins while working in Japan. After trying all of the modern gins, he started tasting samples of older, heavier, and more flavoursome gins—popular in the 1940s and earlier, when gin cocktails were in their heyday—and then approached a specialist London distillery to create something similar. After a long process his ideal recipe emerged. Since he is based in Bermondsey, he named the result Jensen's London-Distilled Dry Bermondsey Gin.

Here, the emphasis is on old-style botanicals and clean, fresh juniper-led flavours that are derived from a small number of classic ingredients such as juniper, coriander, orris root, angelica, and liquorice. Bottled at 43 percent ABV, Jensen's is a taste of what London dry used to be like. Rumour has it that it's a recreation of a once very famous brand—Nicholson's Lamplighter Gin. Its heavier, more aromatic style makes it a good choice for many of the classic gin drinks from the golden age of cocktails.

Jensen's London-Distilled Old Tom Gin is now also available. Its sweeter style is achieved by adding greater quantities of sweet botanicals, not sugar.

JUNIPERO GIN

Made by Anchor Distilling, the guys that kicked off the craft beer movement, Junipero Gin is produced at a craft distillery situated on Portrero Hill in San Francisco. It is a classic dry style of gin made with twelve botanicals in a small copper pot-still. Its makers are coy about the exact ingredients, but tasting reveals strong juniper, liquorice, and grapefruit as well as other citrus. At 49.3 percent ABV, it's a big complex gin with a pronounced spiciness.

LARIOS GIN

Spain is the second largest gin market in the world. There are numerous Spanish-made gin brands, some very local. The only true international brand is Larios, which dominates the domestic market and, indeed, is the fourth biggest gin worldwide. Larios Gin is very much in the London dry style in that is it is double distilled, aromatic and unsweetened with strong juniper flavours evident. For years, there was a question mark over the kind of spirit that Larios was based on. But nowadays the quality is consistently good. Bottled at 40 percent ABV, it is drunk in vast quantities either in a Gin & Tonic or the famous Gin Larios con Coca Cola, which, surprisingly enough, is not half bad. The company recently launched a premium expression: Larios 12, named after its twelve botanicals: juniper, coriander, nutmeg, angelica plus masses of citrus in the form of lemon, orange, mandarin, tangerine, clementine, watermelon, and lime. Here, the spirit and the botanicals are distilled four times and a fifth distillation adds an infusion of orange blossom.

LEOPOLD'S AMERICAN SMALL BATCH GIN

Master Distiller Todd Leopold makes small batches of gin from a unique neutral base of potato, malted barley and summer wheat at the family owned distillery in Denver, Colorado. Using only a 40-gallon pot-still with a six-plate column, each batch of spirit is distilled seven times to gain the purity desired. Then each botanical in the recipe, which includes the peel of Florida oranges and California pomelos, is distilled separately before blending.

The end product comes in an apothecary type bottle with simple white labels and handwritten batch numbers contributing to the gin's lab-sample appearance. At 40 percent ABV this is a superb gin with a robust juniper flavor and the mélange of citrus flavours that so characteriss craft-distilled gins from the United States.

LONDON HILL GIN

The epitome of the London dry style, London Hill Gin is made by whisky experts Ian Macleod Distillers in Scotland. It's made in the traditional way in copper pot-stills and, in addition to the four core botanicals, London Hill also uses cassia, ginger, nutmeg, and liquorice, which give a very rounded profile with juniper just edging it in terms of taste. London Hill gin consistently wins awards at spirit competitions. Yet it's a gin with a very low profile and is not nearly as widely recognised as it deserves to be.

MAGELLAN GIN

French gin, Magellan, is named after the famous sixteenth -century Portuguese explorer Ferdinand Magellan, who led an epic around the world voyage. Although he was killed in the Philippines, his ship returned laden with cloves. A signature botanical of this rather stylishly presented gin, cloves are accompanied by cinnamon, cassia, nutmeg, and grains of paradise alongside the conventional gin botanicals. Made from triple-distilled French wheat spirit that is re-distilled with the botanicals, a final infusion of iris results in a deep blue colour.

MARTIN MILLER'S GIN

The creation of Martin Miller, publisher of the famous Miller's Antique Price Guides, Martin Miller's Gin is made at the Langley Distillery in the Black Country, using traditional methods and craftsmanship. A century-old gem of a copper pot-still named "Angela" is the star of the show. Before distillation, the grain spirit and the botanicals are left to steep overnight in her generous expanse. The botanical recipe is a taste feast with juniper and other common botanicals like coriander, angelica, orange peel and orris root, but also the less often used cassia and cinnamon barks, ground nutmeg, liquorice plus one other secret ingredient, believed to be cucumber. Like all gins, Martin Miller's is reduced with water to its bottling strength of 40 percent ABV. Miller's Gin however takes this to an almost obsessive extreme transporting the elixir on a 3,000-mile round trip to Borganes in Iceland to be blended with what is considered to be the purest water on the planet. Filtered through lava formed millions of years ago, Icelandic glacial water imparts a freshness and smoothness to the taste of Martin Miller's, whilst also contributing greatly to its much-vaunted texture. The end result of all this hard work is a gin that is gentle in the mouth with fragrant, slightly spicy aromas and strong hints of Parma violet and lavender. This unique taste profile makes Martin Miller's the ideal gin for a host of new wave gin drinks with fresh, clean, natural flavours.

MARTIN MILLER'S WESTBOURNE STRENGTH

Named after Martin Miller's original base in Westbourne Grove, West London, Martin Miller's Westbourne Strength Gin is made in exactly the same way as Martin Miller's Gin. Same botanicals, same spirit, same pot-still methods. The major difference is that it is bottled at the much higher 45.2 percent ABV. At this strength, the taste profile veers towards the more classic London flavour with lots of delicious juniper, spice and citrus flavours. The quality of Martin Miller's Westbourne Strength Gin has been recognised by numerous awards in prestigious spirit competitions around the world.

MONKEY 47 GIN

Made by Black Forest Distillers in the heart, yes, of Germany's Black Forest, Monkey 47 is named for its alcoholic strength and the number of botanicals used in its recipe. So it contains all the usual gin botanicals plus some real rarities like spruce tips, blackberries, sloes, sage, and verbena. One third of the ingredients are handpicked in the Black Forest, including fresh cranberries. In the mouth, the spirit seems to be richer and more aromatic that one usually encounters but that could also be down to the sheer volume of the botanical flavourings. Sharp citrus flavours contrast well with pine aromas. It's certainly a good deal fruitier than classic British gins. Aromatic and herbal, Monkey 47 is reminiscent of old style gins where the connection to genever was much stronger than it is today. Which makes it the perfect gin to experiment with in original golden-age cocktails.

NO 3 ST JAMES LONDON DRY GIN

No 3 is produced by iconic spirits company Berry Bros & Rudd and named for the address of the premises founded in 1698 by the Widow Bourne in the heart of London. That original shop is still the oldest wine and spirit merchant in the UK and a mecca for lovers of fine drink.

Made in Schiedam, Holland's distilling centre and gin's ancestral home, No 3 St James is a classic London dry gin bottled at a serious 46 percent ABV. The botanical mix of juniper, coriander, sweet orange peel, angelica, grapefruit peel, and cardamom is left to steep overnight before distillation in traditional copper pot-stills. On the nose there's and instant and welcome hit of piney juniper with citrus and coriander very evident. In the mouth the juniper develops into a crispness nicely balanced by gentle cardamom spiciness. A classic.

NO 209 GIN

No 209 Gin is made at Distillery 209 on Pier 50 in San Francisco. The original 209 Gin Distillery was located on a Napa Valley wine estate that was purchased, in 1999, by food entrepreneur Leslie Rudd. He restored the actual building to its former glory. But its size and location were not suitable for his dream of reviving the distillery, so new premises were purchased in the city and No 209 was reborn.

No 209 Gin is made in a specially commissioned Scottish copper pot-still based on the design of the Glenmorangie whisky stills, which were in fact originally used for making gin. It's a robust gin that is built around the signature botanicals of bergamot, sweet orange, cardamom, and cassia as well as the more usual juniper and citrus. They are macerated in the still overnight and each distillation takes around eleven hours. Unlike most gins, No 209 is not made from concentrated gin that is then reduced with water (aka: the two-shot method). Rather, each single-shot distillation comes off the still ready to be bottled. On the palate, there are very pleasant lavender and floral notes that combine well with the bitter-sweet juniper. A four-times column-distilled spirit made from midwestern corn imparts a smooth, slightly sweet finish. Bartenders recommend No 209 in a Gin Mojito.

OXLEY CLASSIC ENGLISH GIN

This new ultra-premium gin from the Bacardi-owned Oxley Spirits Company was eight years in development. It has certainly brought something new and exciting to the gin scene. In a major technological advance, it is the first ever spirit created by the cold-distillation method. So instead of heat being applied to redistil the spirit with the botanicals, vacuum is used to reduce the pressure in the still and lower the temperature to approximately -5° C. At this temperature the spirit, which has been macerated for 15 hours, becomes vapour. It then meets a cold finger probe (chilled to -100° C) and reverts back to spirit to be collected for bottling.

The bespoke still at London's Thames Distillers produces only 120 bottles per batch. A major advantage of cold distillation is that there are no heads or tails—so it produces less wastage than traditional distillation methods. The most obvious benefit however is the taste of the final product, which is exceptionally clean and fresh. Oxley's 14 botanicals include the traditional flavourings as well as three different types of fresh citrus—grapefruit, orange and lemon—plus exotics like vanilla and meadowsweet. Slightly spicy on the nose with hints of lavender, almond, marshmallow and soft citrus, juniper is evident but not dominant. Think soft and scented rather than oily and pungent. The thing that stands out however is the texture and purity of the spirit that is holding these complex aromas together. At 47 percent ABV, Oxley is a big gin but it's very smooth and lush, almost creamy. It's one of the few gins that one could recommend neat over ice in a balloon glass, ideally with a grapefruit twist.

PLYMOUTH GIN

In the eighteenth century Plymouth, London, Bristol, Warrington, and Norwich were the great gin distilling centres, each producing its own unique style of gin with Plymouth Gin, in particular, having a distinctively aromatic character. Plymouth Gin has remained true to this tradition. Produced in a still which has not been changed for over 150 years, it has a subtle, full bodied flavour with no bitter botanicals and not nearly as much of a juniper hit as some gins. A higher than usual proportion of root ingredients is the source of Plymouth's distinctive, earthy, rooty tastes, whilst the addition of sweet orange and cardamom impart a softly fruity, spicy finish. Pure water from Dartmoor contributes to Plymouth Gin's exceptionally clean and fresh flavour.

Plymouth Gin has a long history, dating back to at least 1793. But the Black Friars building in Plymouth, in which it is made, goes back to the 1400s. There is reason to believe that distilling may have been carried out on these premises as long ago as the sixteenth century. Certainly Black Friars can rightly claim to be the oldest working in distillery in the UK. It is also reputed to have been the place where the Pilgrim Fathers gathered before they set off in the Mayflower, in 1620, for America.

There is a great misconception that Plymouth is an official "style" of gin. It isn't, it's made in exactly the same way as a London dry but it does not carry the London dry label. In fact it's the only UK gin to have a geographic designation a bit like an *appellation controllée*. This does not relate to its production methods but is the result of a series of legal verdicts in the 1880s when a London distiller began producing a "Plymouth" gin. Coates & Co won several suits under the "passing off" legislation, establishing that Plymouth Gin could only be made within Plymouth city walls, by law.

One of the world's great gin brands, Plymouth Gin suffered years of neglect in the hands of the multinationals who never really appreciated its heroic qualities and heritage. But it's now firmly ensconced as a sister brand to Beefeater and Beefeater 24. Plymouth Original is produced at 41.2 percent ABV (83 degrees proof), whilst Plymouth Navy Strength is bottled at a whopping 57 percent ABV. Plymouth also produces a sloe gin and damson gin.

PORTOBELLO ROAD NO 171 GIN

Above the Portobello Star bar along London's famous Portobello Road is the only actual gin museum in London. It's tiny and most importantly also contains the city's smallest working copper pot-still—"Coppernicus". Owners GED Feltham and Jake Burger first experimented with making their own gin in this still. Once they had arrived at a recipe they liked, had it commercially produced at nearby Thames Distillers.

Portobello Road No 171 uses nine botanicals, majoring on warm spice botanicals like cassia bark, liquorice, and nutmeg. Citrus in the form of lemon and bitter orange comes through strongly and somehow, although there is neither cardamom nor grapefruit in the recipe, one picks up hints of aromatic cardamom and grapefruit on the nose. At 42 percent ABV, Portobello comes into its own in tonic water where certain zinginess is required.

RIGHT GIN

The makers of Right Gin deliberately set out to explore gin outside the London style box and have come up with a powerful, unconventional gin. It's made in Sweden from North American corn that is distilled five times, but retains a lingering faint sweetness. The botanicals recipe has juniper, coriander leaf (not the more common seed), cardamom, lemon peel, bergamot, bitter orange, and Sarawak pepper from Borneo. Each botanical ingredient is distilled separately and then combined with the spirit. Pure Swedish water is then used to reduce the gin to 40 percent ABV. Right Gin delivers bold flavours with warm, nutty aromas and lingering pepper notes. It tastes great in the classic cocktails.

ROGUE SPRUCE GIN

Artisanally distilled in Oregon, Rogue Spruce Gin has won numerous awards in prestigious spirits competitions. Made from twelve botanicals that consist of the traditional ones plus spruce oil, whole cucumbers, ginger, grains of paradise, and tangerine. Spruce is a coniferous tree closely related to juniper. So one might think: There's far too much pine going on. But where juniper has a fragrant lavender taste, spruce has a sharper fruitier tang and the combination works. Spruce Gin has a heavy texture with quite a lot of oiliness but clean, tangy evergreen aromas come through nicely. It works particularly well in cocktails like the Bramble or other drinks with dark berries. And it is a great partner for drinks made with sloe gin. There's also a Spruce Pink version, which is aged in Oregon pinot noir barrels, making it slightly fruitier and definitely pink.

SACRED GIN

The Sacred Distillery in London's Highgate is at the heart of the British craft gin movement that is producing excellent gins that have been enthusiastically adopted by London bartenders who also embrace the local food movement. It's made with twelve botanicals including lemon and lime, cardamom, nutmeg, and a very unusual botanical—*Boswellia Sacra* (aka: frankincense) from which the product derives its name.

The distillation process is unusual too as, instead of a traditional copper pot-still, Sacred is made under low pressure vacuum. Each of the twelve botanicals is distilled separately using English grain spirit and then blended to make the final spirit, which is bottled at 40 percent ABV. The theory here is the separate, low pressure, low temperature distillations extract maximum flavour extracted from the botanicals.

On tasting, Sacred is lush and fruity with very big and clean flavours and slightly scented notes derived from the frankincense. It works well with cranberry juice and bitter lemon.

SEAGRAM'S GINS

Seagram's Extra Dry is the US equivalent of Gordon's in the UK—a huge volume brand that outsells its nearest competitors by far. For that reason, it is not appreciated as much as it really ought to be. Known as "the smooth gin in the bumpy bottle", it's made in the USA from 100 percent American grain neutral spirit that is distilled with juniper, coriander, orris, angelica, cardamom, and cassia bark. It is then mellowed in charred white oak barrels, which gives it a slightly golden hue. It has candied fruit, citrus, and juniper on the nose, then a slightly sweet sherbet palate with spice and floral hints and is bottled at 40 percent ABV.

Seagram's Distiller's Reserve is the combination of the best of the barrels as selected out of hundreds by Seagram's Master Distiller. The higher strength of the spirit at 51 per cent ABV is definitely noticeable when sipped straight.

SIPSMITH LONDON DRY GIN

Sipsmith London Dry Gin is produced in a new distillery in London that was once the former office of the late, renowned whisky and beer writer Michael Jackson. The spirit is made by hand in genuinely small batches, never more than 500 bottles a time, often considerably less, by Master Distiller Jared Brown. It is first and foremost, a classic London dry gin, tempered with a touch of the more floral style. The aromas are of citrus and field flower blossoms, balanced with sweet citrus peel, and herbaceous notes reminiscent of a meadow on a warm summer day. On the palate it reveals high quality spirit, distinctive juniper, sweet orange and lemon marmalade, leading to a long, slightly savory finish with a hint of black pepper. This makes it an ideal spirit for a Gin & Tonic or a Gin Collins.

SIX O'CLOCK GIN

Produced by Bramley & Gage who are known for their excellent fruit liqueurs which are made in the heart of the English countryside, Six O' Clock Gin is a breath of fresh air. It's made from seven botanicals – juniper, coriander, angelic, orris, elderflower, orange peel, and savory—which are bottled at a very respectable 43 percent ABV. Exceptionally clean and fresh in the mouth it combines the traditional juniper character of gin with graceful floral notes. Cleverly Bramley & Gage have launched a tonic water to accompany it.

Six O'Clock Tonic is all natural with no saccharin or nasty stuff like sodium benzoate. Instead the bitterness comes from the inclusion of natural quinine extracts plus extracts of lemon and lime. As a result it is clean tasting and not over sweet and goes perfectly with its sister gin.

SLOANE'S GIN

Sloane's Gin is named after Sir Hans Sloane (1660-1753), a Royal Physician, botanist, collector, lifelong benefactor, and landlord of the Physic Garden Chelsea (close to Sloane Square which is also named for him).

Made by blending ten separately distilled botanical distillates, Sloane's Gin combine flavours from across the botanical spectrum – citrus, spice, juniper, floral from the use of iris root, and a musky sweetness from vanilla. The blended gin is then left to settle for a minimum of one month to allow the elements to marry together. At 40 percent ABV the result is a soft, well balanced gin that goes down smoothly.

SW4 GIN

SW4 Gin encapsulates the vision of owner Martin Price who wanted to make a proper old style London dry gin that wouldn't be overpowered by strongly flavoured mixers like tonic or ginger beer.

There are twelve botanicals in the SW4 Gin: the standards plus nutmeg, savory, liquorice, cassia, almond, and lots of citrus with both orange and lemon peel. They are steeped for approximately twelve hours in grain spirit before being distilled in small batches (around 500 liters at a time). Two strengths of SW4 Gin are available: a standard 40 percent ABV and a much stronger version at 47 percent ABV.

In the 40 percent ABV SW4 Gin there is an initial juniper hit followed by citrus and spice with the citrus contributing orange marmalade and lemon curd flavours. As with most classic London dry gins there's a long clean finish with dryness very obvious in the back of the mouth. This is a perfect gin for new-style lemonades.

TANQUERAY GINS

Charles Tanqueray, born in 1810, was the descendant of Huguenots and came from a long line of clergymen. Between 1828 and 1830, he set out to establish himself as a distiller—a choice of profession that would once have been criticised, but distilling was by now something with which a gentleman could be associated. The business of Edward & Charles Tanqueray & Co, Rectifiers was established, by 1838, on Vine Street at the southern edge of Bloomsbury in the parishes of St George, Bloomsbury and St Giles in the Fields. It was known, by 1847, as Charles Tanqueray & Co. However, according to a property deed of the same year, the site had been used as a distillery for some time. A price list of 1895 from W A Taylor & Co of New York illustrates a bottle of Tanqueray's Finest Old Tom, with the caption, "The Bloomsbury Distillery, established 1757".

In his Bloomsbury Distillery, Charles Tanqueray wanted to produce a quality gin. He started with the pure waters of Finsbury spa, a district of rolling countryside and crystal clear streams, then just outside London. After years of experimenting with ingredients, Charles Tanqueray finally produced his unique recipe.

Tanqueray Gin met with instant success and, remaining records show, a small but prestigious clientele. Soon, Tanqueray stoneware crocks—used in the trade until 1900—were to be seen in the better class of grocer plus wine and spirit merchants as well as in discerning households. (He did not deal in bulk-casked gin for ordinary taverns.) Within a few years, Tanqueray Gin exported to the British Colonies while still much in demand at home.

Today, the Tanqueray name is found on three quite different gins. Tanqueray Special Dry Gin is a London dry with knobs on, greeting one boisterously with a lovely juniper fresh welcome. Although the original Tanqueray recipe is still secret, Special Dry is believed to contain only four botanicals, proof that sometimes more is less and that the balance of ingredients is key to its taste. On tasting, juniper and liquorice are very obvious as is a subtle spiciness most likely derived from coriander. At a high-strength 47 percent ABV, based on a clean grain spirit, it is exceptionally dry and somehow very sophisticated. There's also a 43.1 percent ABV version, which is just as good.

Launched in 2000, Tanqueray TEN is a luxury Tanqueray gin bottled at 47.3 percent ABV. Made in small batches, it adds fresh citrus in the form of limes, oranges, and white grapefruit to the botanical mix. The citrus is distilled with pure grain spirit in a swan neck still known as "Tiny Ten". The resulting spirit is then distilled with the more traditional botanicals such as juniper, coriander, angelica, and liquorice. Extra fresh citrus is added to the final spirit. Juniper is at the heart of this gin, but is relatively laid back when compared to big gins like Beefeater and Tanqueray Special Dry. It's very citrusy, clean and as fresh as a meadow with soothing notes of chamomile. Tanqueray TEN was created specifically for Martinis. Owner Diageo has set up the Tanqueray TEN Guild with ten top bartenders from ten cities around the world, who have developed their own signature Martinis. So, for example, Colin Field of the Hemingway Bar at the Ritz Paris freezes both the glass and the Tanqueray TEN to -18.3°C precisely, then adds three olives but no vermouth.

Tanqueray Rangpur is the latest addition to the Tanqueray family. Made with fresh Rangpur limes, juniper, and bay leaf, it is midway between a traditional dry and a fruit gin with a distinctive lime taste. Mix with cranberry juice for a Rangpur Cran or with ginger ale and a few drops of bitters for a Rangpur Ginger.

THE BOTANIST

Another superb offering from Scottish whisky distillers at the Bruichladdich distillery on Islay, The Botanist is termed an "Islay dry gin". It is very much a product of the Hebrides as 21 out of the 31 botanicals used grow on the island itself, including the juniper. The list of native botanicals is almost bewildering, including apple mint birch leaves, bog myrtle leaves, chamomile, thistle flowers, elderflowers, gorse flowers, heather, hawthorn flowers, and mugwort leaves to name but a few. These are added to more traditional gin botanicals and distilled in a low-pressure Lomond pot-still, called "Ugly Betty". It's claimed that the low pressure process helps to release the aromatics from the botanicals.

At 46 percent ABV, The Botanist is a big flavour and very complex gin but retains a strong juniper character despite the number of botanical flavourings used. Clean, bone dry with subtle floral and herbal flavours, it's a winner.

THE LONDON GIN

The London Gin—one of a handful of new-wave gins actually distilled in London—is blue. The colour is derived from gardenia. Its base is a spirit made from Suffolk and Norfolk grain. In line with the classic gins of yesteryear, juniper, coriander, and angelica feature in the recipe of thirteen botanicals, which also includes orris root, orange and lemon peel, liquorice root, savory, cinnamon, and cassia bark. The London Gin throws bergamot into the mix—that instantly recognisable perfumed aroma in Earl Grey tea. Its citric qualities marry well with the fresh juicy flavours of orange and lemon peel, whilst the bergamot also reinforces the "holding" role of orris root. Rested for three weeks after distillation in a pot-still, the result is a very English-style distilled gin. At a generous 47 percent ABV, The London Gin is delicate and elegant on the nose with marked spicy and balsamic notes. Soft, elegant and mellow in the mouth, it's a sophisticated, well-rounded gin that delivers in every area.

VOYAGER GIN

Another US artisan boutique gin from a small family-owned distillery in the Pacific Northwest, Voyager starts life as a Kentucky neutral grain spirit. The botanical recipe of juniper, coriander, licorice, cardamom, anise, lemon, orange, orris, angelica, and cassia is distilled together with the spirit in a small copper pot-still. It is produced in single batches: Each batch makes about thirty 12-bottle cases. Only the heart of the distillation is taken. One point of difference here is that the botanicals are all organic, imported from the best organic growers from around the world. The still-strength spirit is brought down to bottling proof of by adding purified Cascade Mountain water.

WHITLEY NEILL LONDON DRY

Whitley Neill is a premium London dry gin, created by Johnny Neill, the fourth generation of the Greenall Whitley distilling family.

Whitley Neill is a handcrafted gin made from a 100 percent grain spirit that is steeped with the botanicals prior to distillation in antique copper pot-stills. The recipe took some time to formulate as the producers were determined to bring something new to the party. The result is nine botanicals consisting of core botanicals and the addition of two signature elements from Africa—the Cape gooseberry and the fruit of the Baobob tree (aka: the tree of life). The taste experience starts with a spicy freshness on the nose. Laid-back juniper and citrus combine with the fresh tanginess quality of the wild fruit to create robust yet delicate and clean flavours. A pleasant lingering finish holds those flavours in the mouth whilst an alcoholic strength of 42 percent ABV ensures perfect balance.

XORIGEUR GIN, GIN DE MAHON

Xoriguer Gin De Mahon is the only other gin with a geographic destination: It can only be made in Mahon on the Balearic island of Menorca. Gin distilling there dates from the British presence in the eighteenth century when Menorca was an important British base. British soldiers and sailors stationed in Mahon wanted gin, the fashionable spirit at home. Enterprising local distilleries started making it from juniper berries, distilled with a spirit made from the local wine.

The Xoriguer Distillery, founded and still owned by the Pons family, is now the only gin distillery on the island. There, "gin de mahon" is made as it always has been from a wine distillate in ancient copper pot-stills heated by wood burning fires. When it comes off the still it is stored in large oak barrels and bottled at 40 percent ABV.

Only members of the Pons family know the secret of the recipe for Xoriguer. It certainly has juniper and other aromatic herbs. Tasting reveals a brandy-like flavour with notes of caraway, fennel, and orris root. Xoriguer Gin is sold in green-glass bottles with handles that copy the old Dutch stone crocks. It is drunk widely on the island particularly during the summer-long season of fiestas when it is mixed with lemonade in a drink called Pomada. It tastes innocuous. But be warned, it packs a real punch.

ZEPHYR GIN

Named after the Greek god of the west wind, Zephyr is a small-batch distilled gin produced by re-distilling neutral grain spirit with natural botanicals such as juniper berries, citrus peel, and coriander seeds. There are two versions. Black Zephyr uses elderflower and sweet elderberry alongside the more conventional botanicals. Blu Zephyr [yes, it's Blu Zephyr] adds a final infusion of sweet elderberry and gardenia for smoothness and colour. The 40 percent ABV of these gins and their very fruity floral notes create endless possibilities for experimentation in classic and modern cocktails.

ZUIDAM GIN

This high strength 44.5 percent ABV dry gin from the family-owned Zuidam Distillers in Holland is a real gin lover's gin. It contains nine botanicals: juniper berries and iris root from Italy, coriander from Morocco, angelica root, fresh sweet oranges and lemons from Spain, real whole bean vanilla from Madagascar, liquorice root from India, and cardamom pods from Sri Lanka. Unlike most gins that add all the botanicals simultaneously, Zuidam distils each botanical separately and then marries the nine different distillates together according to their secret recipe. Patrick van Zuidam believes that by distilling each element separately, he can extract the purest flavours from the botanicals. The result is a big gin, strong in juniper but with a fiery sweetness. Zuidam also makes an excellent genever gin based on a malt spirit distilled together with juniper, liquorice root, vanilla, aniseed, and marjoram. It's decidedly sweeter than the dry with a malty undertone. Unlike some genevers, it's crystal clear.

FRUIT GINS

All of the old distillers made a vast range of fruit-flavoured gins. Orange and lemon gins lasted well into the twentieth century. But the fashion for fruit gins seems to have largely disappeared with one notable exception—sloe gin.

Sloe gin is described as a "British liqueur". It's made by steeping wild sloe berries, the fruit of the blackthorn tree, in gin and allowing the flavours to marry. Once the favourite drink of prim Victorian ladies and the "tweed clad", sloe gin has made the leap from the hip flasks of the hunting, fishing, and shooting set to the backs of the most stylish bars. There's now a raft of new ways of drinking sloe gin in cocktails and long drinks that tie in with the fashion for drinking seasonally, using locally-sourced ingredients.

Try it with English apple juice, garnished with an apple slice. Or add 25 ml of sloe gin to champagne or sparkling wine for an apéritif that not only tastes great but also looks very pretty. Sloe gin is also delicious on its own: An excellent alternative to brandy or port as an after-dinner drink.

Gordon's, Plymouth, and Sipsmith make sloe gin. Another traditional brand, Hawker's Sloe Gin, has come back into production. Many rural food producers and farm shops have also got in on the act producing excellent sloe gins. However sloe gin is easy to make at home.

Gather your sloe berries. Old railway lines are a good source for some reason. Fill a gin bottle half way with sloes, add 2 inches of castor sugar and top up with full-strength gin. Leave for several weeks to mature. Shake the bottle every now and again, if you remember, and there it is.

FRUIT CUPS

The famous Pimm's No 1 Fruit Cup was invented by James Pimm in London in 1840. He owned a chain of restaurants all over the City and made a gin drink blended with liqueurs, herbs, and spices that he sold to his customers in pint tankards. In 1859, he started bottling it for sale to other bars and restaurants. The company was sold to Sir Horatio Davis, a city entrepreneur, who developed an export trade for Pimm's. One of the first-recorded exports was to the famous Galle Face Hotel in Colombo, Sri Lanka. Pimm's was also sent up the Nile, in 1898, to the forces at Khartoum and Omdurman in the Sudan.

Other Pimm's cups were introduced, based on scotch whisky (No 2), brandy (No 3), rum (No 4), rye whiskey (No 5) and vodka (No 6). But the gin-based Pimm's No 1 remains the taste of English summer.

DUTCH GENEVER

If you're a fan of Dutch genever, a visit to Schiedam, just outside Rotterdam, is an absolute must. The town is as important to Dutch spirits as the Scottish Highlands is to whisky. In 1880, Schiedam boasted 392 distilleries and its economy was entirely based around genever, with hundreds of cooperages, brass and cork factories, malt houses, yeast makers and glass works. Twenty huge windmills, the largest in the world, ground grain to feed the stills. The Museum of Genever in Schiedam is crammed with information and also has a working distillery making traditional, maltwine genever.

Although Dutch genever is no longer the fashionable drink it once was, there are still over 200 brands on the market, including fruit-flavoured ones. Many are small local brands. Large producers like Bols and De Kuypers make the biggest brands.

Bols is the oldest distilling firm in Holland and, at its vast premises in Zoetermeer, makes a number of different types of genever, including the recently launched Bols Genever in its stylish modern packaging.

De Kuyper was founded in 1695 and still produces an excellent jonge graanjenever and an oude genever, but is now better known for its vast range of liqueurs.

There are also interesting craft genever brands like Zuidam and those made by AV Wees that are attracting attention from the bartending fraternity.

THE GREAT GIN DRINKS

Whilst there are many ways to drink gin, this book will confine itself to the all time classics and some modern variations. And, since it's not a cocktail book as such, concentrates on telling the stories behind most them.

THE GIN & TONIC

Gin & Tonic is as quintessentially English as bacon and eggs or tea and cucumber sandwiches. With the sharp, piney flavour of juniper balancing the bitter sweetness of tonic, it's so perfect a match one would almost think they had been invented with each other in mind. But each half of this iconic partnership has its own quite distinctive story.

Like gin, tonic water began life as a medicine, its principal flavour derived from quinine bark, the well-known antidote to malaria. Reputedly, it all started in Peru, in 1638, when the wife of the Spanish viceroy, Countess Chinchona, was cured of fever by a local medicine man using the bark of the native quina tree. Legend has that, in gratitude, she vowed to make her miraculous healing widely known. On her return to Spain, she took quantities of the bark back to the family estate at Chinchon, outside Madrid (where the town of Chinchon still exists). The fame of this magical substance that we know as quinine—but is botanically named *cinchona officinalis*, in honour of the Countess—spread throughout Europe. Used to cure both Charles II of England and the son of Louis XIV of France, the powdered bark became more precious than gold and just as hard to come by.

The trade in quinine bark was dominated by countries like Bolivia and Peru where chinchona, the "fever tree", grew naturally. In the 1850s British and Dutch explorers began to smuggle seeds out of Latin America and planted cinchona trees in their tropical colonies: the British in India and Ceylon. Unfortunately they did not produce the quality of quinine necessary. Finally the Dutch established plantations in Java with seeds taken from Bolivia. These did produce the required standard of quinine. By 1918 the Dutch controlled the world's supply.

Quinine was prescribed to both prevent and treat malaria and the bark was urgently needed throughout the tropics where malaria was rife. The British in India masked the bitter flavour of quinine with sugar and diluted the mixture with water to make it drinkable in the daily doses given to soldiers and other functionaries of the British Raj. It wasn't long before some bright spark realised that gin would enliven the medicine and the ideal sundowner was born.

Returning expats brought the taste for this exotic drink home with them where it became known as "Indian tonic water". Commercial production of "tonic brewed drinks" began in the nineteenth century. They were usually a combination of quinine salt that was rendered soluble in citric acid, which was blended with other bitter ingredients such as cassia or gentian, chiretta, and horehound. One of the first to market was the "improved aerated tonic liquid" which was patented, in 1858, by Erasmus Bond.

Dutch domination of the quinine trade continued until the Second World War when the Japanese occupied Java. The resulting shortage of quinine for medicinal purposes drove the quest to develop a synthetic version of the quinine alkaloid. By 1944 scientists had synthesized quinine and pharmaceutical companies were able to produce various quinine-based drugs. At the same time plantations of natural chinchona were successfully established in parts of Africa.

Most modern commercially produced tonic waters are based on synthetic quinine and hence taste quite different to the original Indian tonic water: particularly in the US where tonic water tends to be much sweeter and usually contains dreaded high-fructose corn syrup.

There's been a bit of a backlash against this. Over the past few years many excellent authentic tonic waters that do contain natural quinine and—like the original tonic waters—other botanical ingredients have come onto the market. In the UK the best are Fentimans, Fevertree; in the US, Q Tonic leads.

The Perfect Gin & Tonic

You wouldn't think it was necessary to give instructions for this very common drink but the G&T has been very badly let down by pub bartenders who serve it too weak, with not enough ice and flat tonic water from a gun. Made properly and drunk at the right time a Gin & Tonic is the perfect drink. Follow these simple rules:

- Always use a good quality gin.
- Use a single serve bottle or can of tonic water.
- Take a tall glass with a heavy bottom, which makes the bubbles in the tonic, last longer. Fill it with ice (at least four large cubes) and add a generous measure of gin. Pour in enough tonic to fill the glass. What you're aiming for is just over double the amount of tonic to gin.
- Add a freshly cut wedge of lemon or lime and rub it around the rim of the glass first. Some gin fans claim that lemon or lime spoils the flavour of the more citrus gins. *Chacun a sa gout.* Stir gently with a teaspoon or a cocktail stirrer.

THE DRY MARTINI

Only one thing can be said about the Dry Martini—the King of Cocktails—without provoking a storm of debate: It is American, and, as the humorist HL Mencken described, it is "the only American invention as perfect as the sonnet." Venturing into the Martini debate is a minefield as there are so many conflicting stories concerning its origins. Some say it evolved from the Martinez, first made at the time of the Gold Rush in Martinez, California in 1862.

The Martinez recipe specifies red vermouth, Old Tom gin, bitters, and maraschino cherry juice so crucially one of the first unions of gin and vermouth has been made, if the date is correct. Others claim the creator of the Martini to be Signor Martini di Arma di Taggia, a bartender in New York's Knickerbocker Hotel. The most credible explanation comes from drinks historians Anistasia Miller and Jared Brown who date the popularity of the mix of gin and dry (aka: white) vermouth to the turn of the twentieth century when the Italian Martini & Rossi company was promoting heavily its new "extra dry vermouth". It seems more than likely therefore that the drink we know took its name from the brand.

With the increasing domination of dry gin, the formula became established as the one we know today: gin, dry vermouth, an olive or a twist of lemon. Then the debate moved on to the exact proportions of the ingredients with some proposing a 7:1 gin to vermouth ratio whilst others advocated 4:1. Hard-core Martini fans like Spanish filmmaker Luis Bunuel "simply allowed a ray of sunlight to shine through a bottle of Noilly Prat before it hits the bottle of gin." Winston Churchill apparently just bowed in the direction of France as he measured his Plymouth Gin into a glass with an olive.

Nowadays, the fashion for Dry Martinis is very dry indeed. Even though minute quantities of vermouth are used, a Gin Martini made this way still tastes remarkably different from neat gin with an olive.

The recipe for two Gin Martinis is simple, yet precise:

Into a cold metal shaker filled with ice pour 1 tablespoon dry vermouth to coat the ice. Strain off the excess vermouth and pour in 7oz [210 ml] of gin. Stir until ice cold. Then strain into two cold cocktail glasses. Either zest the oil from 2 strips of lemon peel over each glass or garnish each drink with a single olive. A small, pickled cocktail onion makes it a Gibson.

Ask for a Dry Martini in a bar and the bartender will practically hug you as mixing a Martini is the ultimate test of cocktail skill. Everyone has his or her own theories. It's also a bit of a test of drinking skill and should be approached with caution. As the old joke goes "the Martini is like a woman's breasts because one is not enough and three's too many". Or as Dorothy Parker quipped:

I like to have a Martini
Two at the very most
After three I'm under the table
After four I'm under the host

Or as her fellow member of the famous Algonquin Round Table (aka: The Vicious Circle) Ogden Nash put it:

There's something about a Martini,
A tingle remarkably pleasant;
A yellow, a mellow Martini;
I wish I had one at present.
There is something about a Martini,
Ere the dining and dancing begin,
And to tell you the truth,
It is not the vermouth—
I think that perhaps it's the gin.

But possibly the best descriptions of the effect a perfect Dry Martini can have is to be found in the writing of the comic master PG Wodehouse and his marvellous creations, Bertie Wooster and Jeeves. One of the funniest comes at the beginning of *Jeeves and The Feudal Spirit* when Bertie Wooster is steeling himself to reveal the moustache he has grown during Jeeves annual holiday in Bognor Regis. Only a Jeeves special Martini will help him get his nerve up.

"…. Mere Martinis, I felt, despite their numerous merits, would not be enough to see me through the ordeal that confronted me. It was in quite fairly tense mood that I dried and clothed the person, and while it would perhaps be too much to say, as I entered the sitting room some quarter of an hour later, that I was a-twitter, I was unquestionably conscious of certain jumpiness. When Jeeves came in with the shaker I dived at like a seal going after a slice of fish and drained a quick one, scarcely pausing to say, 'Skin off your nose'.

"The effect was magical. That apprehensive feeling left me. To be succeeded by a quiet sense of power. I cannot put it better than by saying that, as the fire coursed through my veins, Wooster the timid fawn became in a flash Wooster the man of iron will, ready for anything. What Jeeves inserts in these specials of his I have never ascertained but their morale-building force is extraordinary. They wake the sleeping tiger in a chap. Well, to give you some idea, I remember once after a single one of them striking the table with clenched fist and telling my Aunt Agatha to stop talking rot. And I'm not sure it wasn't 'bally rot'."

For many Martini fans however, the Dry Martini is the Little Black Dress of the cocktail world. You don't wear it every day. You don't even wear it at every party. But as soon as you've got it on, you know that it was the right choice.

THE NEGRONI

The Negroni is *la dolce vita* in a glass, summoning up images of all that is best about the Italian way of life. It's an exquisitely simple drink that real gin lovers love and it's one of the few classic cocktails whose provenance can be traced to a specific time and place. Imagine the scene: the Bar Casoni in Florence, circa 1920, where patrons are enjoying their Americanos, a drink made with Campari, sweet vermouth, and soda water, named thus because of pro-American feelings after World War I. The Americano was the most fashionable drink of the day. But one regular had his own ideas about what made the perfect apéritif. Every day, Count Camillo Negroni ordered his Americano to be made with gin without soda water. Soon his friends began to request their drinks "the Negroni way." A classic was born.

Unlikely as it seems this story is almost certainly true. Count Negroni certainly existed and there are numerous photographs of him in the excellent work *Sulle Tracce del Conte* by Luca Picchi. He led a colourful life, having been a cowboy and a professional gambler in the USA in his youth.

The fame of his invention spread throughout the bars and grand hotels of Florence and then became the favourite drink of the Italian Futurists, the avant-garde literary and artistic movement led by Filippo Tommaso Marinetti. It has had many famous fans including Orson Welles, who discovered the Negroni while filming *Black Magic* in Rome in 1947. His verdict: "The bitters are excellent for your liver, the gin is bad for you. They balance each other."

Today, along with many other gin cocktails from the Great Cocktail Age of the 1920s, the Negroni has become ultra-fashionable again. Partly that is to do with its authenticity, partly too because, like the Martini, it's a drinker's drink. As Kingsley Amis, one of alcohol's great heroes, said: "This is a really fine invention. It has the power, rare with drinks and indeed with anything else, of cheering you up."

The recipe could not be more simple and goes like this:

Equal parts of gin, Campari and red vermouth such as Cinzano or Martini Rosso. (Although bartenders do like to play with more aromatic vermouths like Punt e Mes.)

Combine all the ingredients in mixing glass filled with ice. Stir gently and pour into an old-fashioned glass. Add a hefty orange slice as a garnish.

PINK GIN

Traditionally the drink of officers and gentlemen, "Pinkers—as it is known amongst sailors—is a very British drink that came about as a result of the drinking habits of the Royal Navy. A Royal Navy ship's surgeon first used a combination of Angostura bitters, gin, and a splash of water as a cure for seasickness and fatigue on board long sea voyages and the drink caught on. In Britain it is more generally known as Pink Gin whilst in former British colonies it was known as Gin Pahit (the word *pahit* means "bitter" in Malay) and the addition of tiny onions marinated in chilli makes it a Gin Piaj. Whatever its name, drinking this drink once instantly identified you as a navy man or a colonial.

References to it abound in the writing of Somerset Maugham, that great chronicler of British colonial life. In his short story "P. & O.," a rubber farmer named Gallagher from Galway returns home after 25 years working on a Malay rubber plantation. On board ship, he has a drink with a woman he has just met: "the Irishman ordered a Dry Martini for her and a Gin Pahit for himself. He had lived too long in the East to drink anything else."

It's not a drink for the faint hearted.

2 dashes Angostura bitters
1 part gin
1 part water
Swirl several drops of Angostura bitters around in a tumbler-type glass. Shake out the residue. Add the gin and water. No ice. Remember: it's British.

THE GIMLET

This very simple combination of gin and Rose's Lime Cordial also has a strong connection to the Royal Navy and dates back to 1867 when Lachlan Rose, a Scottish chandler based in Edinburgh, came up with a formula to preserve citrus fruit juice without using alcohol. It was invaluable because scurvy, caused by a deficiency of vitamin C, was still a major danger for sailors on long sea voyages. With superb timing, that same year a law required all vessels, Royal Navy and merchant alike, to carry limes not lemons to be given daily ration to the crews. This led to the remarkable success of Rose's Lime Cordial and along the way resulted in British sailors being called "limeys".

The Gimlet is reputedly named after a naval surgeon, Dr Gimlette, who persuaded his fellow officers to mix their daily ration of Rose's with gin.

It was also the favourite drink of Philip Marlowe, Raymond Chandler's ultra cool private detective hero. In his novel *The Long Goodbye*, Philip Marlowe and a playboy named Terry Lennox bond over Gimlets at Victor's bar:

"We sat in the corner bar at Victor's and drank Gimlets. 'They don't know how to make them here,' he said. 'What they call a gimlet is just some lime or lemon juice and gin with a dash of sugar and bitters. A real Gimlet is half gin and half Rose's Lime Juice and nothing else. It beats Martinis hollow."

Here's the recipe:

1 part gin
1 part Rose's Lime Cordial (it really doesn't work with fresh lime juice)
Pour ingredients into a mixing glass three quarters filled with ice cubes. Stir until ice cold. Strain into a chilled martini glass. Garnish with a slice of lime peel.

THE WHITE LADY

This drink was invented during the Great Cocktail Age of the 1920s by Scottish bartender, Harry MacElhone, initially at Ciro's in London where the original recipe specified crème de menthe not gin. In 1923 Harry purchased the famous New York Bar in Paris where in 1929, he perfected the recipe below.

2 shots [50 ml] gin
3/4 shot [18.75 ml] Cointreau
3/4 shot [18.75 ml] freshly-squeezed lemon juice
1/4 shot [6.25 ml] sugar syrup
1/2 egg white
Shake with ice, strain into a chilled cocktail glass and garnish with a lemon twist.

Harry's New York Bar was the watering hole of the expat American artistic community who lived in Europe in the period between the two World Wars. F Scott Fitzgerald and Ernest Hemingway were habitués. Hence the oft repeated canard that it was they who invented the White Lady. Composer George Gershwin worked on his "An American in Paris Suite" in the downstairs piano bar. Other notable guests over the years included Humphrey Bogart and the Duke of Windsor.

A 1960 Ian Fleming short story "From a View to Kill" gives a flavour of the Harry's New York Bar experience. It has James Bond visiting Harry's Bar during his first visit to Paris at age sixteen. He followed the instructions in Harry's advertisement in the Continental Daily Mail and ordered his taxi driver to 'Sank Roo Doe Noo'. He recalls "That had started one of the memorable evenings of his life, culminating in the loss, almost simultaneous, of his virginity and his notecase".

NEW WAVE GIN COCKTAILS

Most of the great classic cocktails were originally invented as gin drinks. Nowadays, as they have rediscovered gin, bartenders love to play with it and experiment with the different flavours that different botanical profiles provide. Some of the new style gins particularly those with floral and spicy notes suit new-wave recipes like the ones below:

The Bramble

(Invented by Dick Bradsell)
2 shots [50 ml] gin
1 shot [25 ml] fresh-squeezed lemon juice
1/2 shot [12.5 ml] simple syrup
1/2 shot [12.5 ml] crème de mures
Shake the first three ingredients over ice and strain into an old-fashioned glass filled with crushed ice. Slowly drizzle the crème de mure through the crushed ice to create a "marbled effect" and garnish with blackberries and a lemon slice.

Lime and Coriander Martini

2 shots [50 ml] gin
1/2 shot [12.5 ml] freshly squeezed lime juice
1/2 shot [12.5ml] simple syrup
12 - 15 leaves fresh coriander
Muddle the coriander leaves with lime juice and simple syrup. Add the gin and fill the shaker with ice. Shake, then double strain into a cocktail glass. Rim glass with a piece of sliced fresh chilli, then drop it into the glass.

Crimson Fizz

2 shots [50 ml] gin
1 tablespoon simple syrup
6 fresh strawberries
soda water
Muddle the strawberries into a shaker. Add remaining ingredients and ice. Shake vigorously for several minutes, and then strain into a cold collins or fizz glass. Fizz up with bottled soda water, stirring continuously as the water is added. The point of this drink is that it should be served foamy and fizzy.

Elderflower Collins

(A new version of the classic Collins)
2 shots [50 ml] gin
2 shots [50 ml] lemon juice
1/2 shot [12.5 ml] elderflower cordial
1/2 shot [12.5 ml] simple syrup
Build all of the ingredients in the glass. Stir well with a bar spoon. Fizz up with bottled soda water, stirring continuously as water is added. Add ice.

Waterloo Sunset

(A reworking of the classic champagne cocktail by Dan Warner)
3/4 shot [approx 20 ml] gin
1/2 shot [12.5 ml] elderflower cordial
4 shots [100 ml] Perrier Jouët champagne
1/4 shot [6 ml] créme de framboise
Stir gin and elderflower cordial in a bar glass or shaker filled with ice. Strain into a flute glass. Using the spiral of a bar spoon layer the champagne on top. Then layer the crème de framboise with a bar spoon. Garnish with a speared raspberry.

Bittered Sling

35 ml gin
10 ml Mandarine Napoleon liqueur
25 ml elderflower cordial
25 ml freshly squeezed lemon juice
10 ml Bénédictine
soda water

Shake all ingredients, except the soda water, over ice and strain into a sling glass filled with cubed ice. Top up with soda water and garnish with fresh apple slices.

INDEX

A

B

C

D

E

F

G

H

J

K

L

W

X

Y

Z

Lightning Source UK Ltd.
Milton Keynes UK
UKOW06f2221151117
312783UK00001B/306/P